Through writing to reading

Children of all abilities, but especially those who have trouble learning to read, can be greatly helped if they first understand what it feels like to be 'a reader'. In this inspiring and very practical book for teachers, support teachers and other classroom helpers, Brigid Smith shows how children's own words, dictated to an adult and then read back, can give them this initial experience of literacy. At the same time, the process of reading encourages the children to edit their work, thus practising compositional skills which would otherwise be beyond their reach. From their success in this, teachers can gradually guide them towards the skills needed to decode unfamiliar text.

Brigid Smith explains how teachers can use this approach in their own classrooms with different kinds of texts, with individuals and with groups and with children with all levels of reading difficulty, including dyslexics. While her emphasis is on enjoyment and independence for the reader, she also shows how the method she suggests can fulfil the requirements of the National Curriculum and how progress can be monitored for assessment purposes. The book is illustrated throughout with case studies and examples of children's writing.

Brigid Smith is Senior Lecturer in Education at Homerton College, Cambridge, and, with Margaret Peters, the author of *Spelling in Context* (1993).

Through writing to reading

Classroom strategies for supporting literacy

Brigid Smith

London and New York

First published 1994
by Routledge
11 New Fetter Lane, London EC4P 4EE

Simultaneously published in the USA and Canada
by Routledge
29 West 35th Street, New York, NY 10001

Reprinted 1997

Typeset in Palatino by LaserScript, Mitcham, Surrey
Printed and bound in Great Britain by
Biddles Ltd, Guildford and King's Lynn

British Library Cataloguing in Publication Data
A catalogue record for this book is available from the British Library

Library of Congress Cataloguing in Publication Data
Smith, Brigid.
  Through writing to reading: classroom strategies for supporting
  literacy / Brigid Smith.
  p. cm.
  Includes bibliographical references and index.
  1. Reading – Language experience approach. 2. English language –
  Composition and exercises – Study and teaching. 3. Storytelling.
  I. Title.
  LB1050.35.S65 1994
  372.4 – dc20   93-34387
                                                           CIP

ISBN 0–415–09613–8 (hbk)
ISBN 0–415–09614–6 (pbk)

Contents

Figures

Introduction

There is a common bridge for a child of any race and of more
moment than any other: the bridge from the inner world outward
Sylvia Ashton-Warner in *Teacher* (1963)

This book is the result of ten years' work in classrooms and with learners
of all kinds and of all ages. It all started with the attempt to help some
Year 7 children to read who were finding the task almost impossible.
Together we spluttered and agonised over thin, bent cornered books
whose artificial language and content failed to engage any of us in the
activity of reading pleasurably and with intent. It was in desperation one
day that I took up my pen and said to 11-year-old John,

"Tell me a story and I'll write it down."

John told me the story of Bad Jim, the Rolls Royce Robber. John was unable
to read although he had a clear idea of how he should do it in his head:

"I sounds it out Miss. Everytime I sounds it out I get it wrong."

How was it possible to reverse such a firm conviction of failure? Between
the lines of the first chapter of his book it is possible to hear the questions
that encouraged each new sentence.

Once upon a time there was a man who had four Rolls Royces.
He was very rich.
He lived in a mansion. One day he had these four Rolls Royces stolen. He went
to the police station.
He told them he had four Rolls Royces stolen.

John read this text the first time it was typed and returned to him with
increasing fluency and confidence. He could read the whole page and he
was delighted. This book and another were composed and read and it is
interesting to look at the language of Chapter One of a third book, *The
Great Escape*, in which Bad Jim is serving time.

One morning Bad Jim the Rolls Royce Robber found a saw. It was baked into a cake that the Butler had made for Jim. It was a birthday cake shaped like a saw. It was covered with pink icing and the candles were really dynamite sticks. Bad Jim cut the cake and he found the saw and dynamite sticks and he is relieved. At last he can get out of jail. He didn't like the jail much because he didn't get much food. Most of all he wanted some chicken and bread pudding washed down with Coke.

Here it is possible to see a reader and composer who has found that reading can be fun and who has a sense of power over words and of real achievement in producing a written text. John was on the way to being a real reader. Initial informal attempts to create reading texts were merely such requests to pupils to 'tell me a story' and that story, written down, then being used as a book to read.

Yesterday I received a letter in the post dictated by my 3-year-old grand-daughter, Hannah, and typed by her father.

I've been outside playing with my bike. We've been working on the bike and we went to Cyrils to talk to him. . . we saw a goose in the hedge and she was sitting on her eggs.

The story she sent me the other day has the same immediacy of remembered events, caught in words, and now transcribed for someone else to read:

We rescued the sheep out the brambles. My trousers was wet. I took them off.

She expects the story to be returned, made into a book and typed for her to read in my bold Apple Mac print, her own words achieving the same status as *Peace at Last* or any other of her well-loved books. She expects that her grandfather and I will reply to her letter telling her our news and responding to her communication:

A goose! How wonderful! We've only seen eggs in the shops here.

She and John are engaged in the same activity: making sense of their world in words and encapsulating that world of thought and action in a text that they can read or that can be read to them. They are learning the difference between talking and talk written down for reading. Soon, no doubt, Hannah will learn that the way you write a letter has more to do with talk than with the kind of writing that you find between the cover of a book. This is the Language Experience approach which has been used in infant schools for many years. Children have the 'story' of their picture written underneath it. Such dictated texts can be used as an important and effective part of their reading programme and children's own stories can now be found in the reading corners of many primary schools.

My own attempts to use this approach with pupils who were finding reading and writing difficult at the point of transfer to secondary school seemed to produce an increase in their interest and confidence in reading. It became an activity in which helpers in the school were encouraged to take part. At one point 27 adults, sixth formers, fifth year truants, mothers and others were writing down texts for pupils and listening to them reading them. The books that were produced were merely typed A5 sheets held together with a plastic spiral which easily allowed additional pages to be added. It soon became clear that some pupils were finding in their own texts stories to read which interested them in a way which no commercial text could. Stories about fishing and winning fishing competitions were popular reading.

Justine was a familiar kind of non-reader; all books were 'boring'. However, her own dictated stories, *My Sister's Wedding* and *My Sister's Baby*, elicited enthusiasm and animated reading in a way that no book had previously achieved. The beginning of *My Sister's Wedding* may give an indication of the reason for this:

> *Once upon a time I was a bridesmaid.*
> *It was in January.*
> *My sister Sharon was getting married to Peter.*
> *They were married in church.*
> *It was a great big church.*
> *My grandad took a bottle of whiskey to the church and while my sister was saying all the words he was drinking it.*

The book is full of details of dresses and hairstyles and scraps between the bridesmaids and the brother who only wanted to see the football. Readers who need encouraging want to meet themselves, their interests, their own language in a book. When they do they get a new perception of what reading and stories are about.

Other pupils too began to find Margaret Meek's 'imaginative drive to cognitive function'[1] through composing and reading their own stories. Clive wrote a story which fictionalised his own life. In a 32-chapter book he explored his own life and then internalised some of his fears, anxieties and traumas in a fast-moving story encompassing school and children's home.[2]

Trying to find stories which would meet the needs of traveller children, coming to school and formal literacy late but bringing with them the richness of an oral story tradition, confirmed the importance of an approach which built on the language of the reader. Jessie entitled her first book *Stories of Olden Days*, a literary enough title, and it contained short, fast-moving versions of stories told by her grandad and uncles when they 'Come up and talk about the olden days'. Her story of the washing has an individual flavour and a use of language which would not be possible to find in a reading book.

> *When my Aunts and Uncles were stopping in this field these cranky men come around the trailers. My Uncle Joey and all the rest of the men go out and tried to get the men away. As soon as my Uncle Joey comed out of the trailer with the men they all runned away. My Uncle Joey bumped into my Aunt Cissie's washing and he thought it was a man!*
> *He yelled, 'He's got me' and he started beating the washing with a lump of wood. My Aunt Cissie busted out of laughing.*

Jessie was able to use her oral language to make sense of a text on the page. Her use of dialect in 'comed' and 'busted out of laughing' means that her own syntax can help her to read the text. In another traveller's text there is a more specific example of the way in which dialect can help in making printed text familiar and accessible:

> *Violet never ate her dinner. She gave it to the nanny goat.*
> *Here mother said, 'I dare you, you naughty girl.*
> *You govit the milk.*
> *You govit the biscuits.*
> *You govit your dinner.*
> *What you doing to give it next?'*

No carefully graded and repetitive reader is likely to produce such a compelling text for a beginning reader who, at the stage of dictating and writing this story, couldn't write her own name.

Here are stories which are motivating and relevant to their readers. They are 'real reads' in the sense that the reader has to read complete texts with longer sentences and more complicated vocabulary than they are likely to meet in initial reading texts. If they make a mistake they are likely to know that their reading is incorrect because they already know the story and can match the prediction with the meaning in the story.[3] John was able to 'sound it out' and get it right because he already had a good idea of what the word might be likely to be and could use his phonic analysis in a positive and meaningful way.[4]

Later I had the oppporunity to try this way into reading again – in primary special schools, in infant and junior schools, amongst 'leavers' classes of non-examination pupils seeing out the long last days of school. In all the cases a kind of magic occurred when the triangle of composer, scribe and text was established and the act of composing, reading, editing and reflecting took place.

Working in India as a language consultant in a British Council Project I realised how essential such approaches are when reading and writing materials are limited or non-existent. There it is necessary that anything that is written on a precious piece of paper should be able to be used as reading materials for others. In this way a sense of audience, purpose and context in writing begins to make the literacy process one which is grounded in real learning and meaningful activities.

The National Curriculum for English endorses the use of relevant reading materials which relate to the reader's own interests. The use of scribing as a support for readers who find the task of reading difficult is encouraged, and reading and writing books for others to read is a component of the programmes of study at Key Stage 1 and 2. The more subtle aspects of literacy knowledge – the difference between oral and written discourse, the ability to reflect on their own writing and the reader/writer overlap – are all part of knowledge about language in the National Curriculum. These areas are spelled out in detail for those teachers who wish to see how reading and writing dictated stories can be related to the National Curriculum and assessed in this way.

Helping children to create a bridge between their own oral language and the 'frozen'[5] language of text is achieved through producing materials that are low in cost but that give a high status to the composer/reader. The pleasure I found in seeing reluctant and passive readers and writers composing and reading their own texts enthusiastically led me into the thickets of research – I needed to look more closely at what was happening and to pin down, so that it could acquire a respectable genesis, this text called 'the dictated story'. I also had a number of questions in my head which had arisen from teachers' queries and hesitations when I had talked about children learning to read in this way. My own experience of using non-professionals to help in the scribing of the books and in listening to them being read needed to be properly organised and assessed. These questions formed the basis of two classroom-based research projects[6] and are the framework of the chapters in this book. The research was intended to answer the following specific questions:

1 How could teachers use this approach in a busy classroom when it required individual attention?
2 If non-professional helpers were used, as suggested, how could the teachers be sure that they were listening to reading in a way acceptable to the teacher?
  What did the helper do in the interaction between composer/reader and scribe/listener?
3 Did reading behaviour change as a result of pupils reading their own stories written down?
4 Were the stories that were dictated 'real' texts?
5 Was the discourse of the text and the structure of the story more like talking or more like writing?
6 What was a dictated story anyway?

I hope that I am now able to answer these questions with confidence and clarity after the years which I spent looking, questioning and analysing on my own account. By its very nature research focuses on micro features; but, through detailed examples and analysis, illumination and understanding can be given to a broader sweep of educational activity. It has always been my intention that the results of this research should be available for teachers to use in their classrooms, and this book contains many examples of practical ways of using dictated stories with a variety of learners. The analysis of features of dictated story discourse and the structure of a dictated story are examined in some detail in chapters 4 and 5 and the examples relate directly to the sample group. This focus allows insight into the extent to which a dictated story is able to act as a bridge text between a reader's oral language and written text. Features of written text identified in the research are also seen as ways in which teachers could evaluate elements within the dictated text that relate to progress in learning to be a writer. Suggestions for assessing and recording progress are given in Chapter 8.

From the evidence in the research this book describes the nature of the dictated story, how children read such stories and the way in which the dictated texts are composed in interaction with a scribe. Further details are given in the Notes to enable other researchers and teachers interested in looking more closely at their own practice to follow the threads of the research itself. The photocopiable materials in the ap- pendices should enable any teacher to support a helper in their classroom to work with a child composing and reading their own books.

I still find this activity the most rewarding and enjoyable way of helping and supporting a learner reader. I hope others will be persuaded not only of the pleasure of the task but also of its value and importance as an interim step in enabling many children to become good readers and, ultimately, writers.

Chapter 1

Learning to read
The context for questions

In order to focus on the specific questions it is important to see the place of this approach to learning to read in the history and theory of reading. This context becomes particularly cogent because we are now in the middle of contentious arguments about the teaching of reading. This central issue in primary classrooms and matter for concern when there are literacy difficulties has been politicised and given a polarised focus by the media. The debate all too often resolves into a simplistic argument about teaching methods, though, as teachers know, and HMI reports[1] have confirmed, what teachers usually do in practice is to use a variety of methods and approaches which are matched to the needs of individual learners. These methods are, however, now subsumed under a wider understanding of the ways in which language works and the ways in which children learn.

The previous 'great debate' was focused solely on methodology until the understanding of psycholinguistics emphasised the importance of purpose, context and understanding in the experience of learning to read and write. Reading began to be regarded as a whole language activity in which context, prediction and meaning were as important as the structure of the sentence or the discrete parts of the words. Recent psychological studies of reading[2] have shown that children need to know what a whole text means and to experience how it hangs together before they are ready to deal with discrete parts and make sense of them. Developmental levels also make some aspects of reading more accessible to the reader. The background to this research has been a view of reading as a part of a whole language experience; and of reading instruction as being con-textualised in real life meanings and purposes. The whole language of the child is important when they are learning to read. When children ex-perience difficulties the emphasis has shifted from giving remedial help to the child to producing materials which support, motivate and extend the reader, in this way reinforcing the approaches used with beginning readers.

What teachers know is that books can be particularly inaccessible to pupils lacking experience of literary language, for the first-time learners find their oral language ineffective and unacceptable. It becomes clear that reading schemes, however well graded, are not sufficient for such beginning readers and that these children require considerable experience of what books are like and what reading is about. Many children now come to a knowledge of literacy through access to books which introduce reading in collaborative and enjoyable ways, emphasising rhythm and rhyme, reading in shared and unstressful situations. These children view themselves as readers and practise reading-like behaviour from their earliest days in school.[3] Opportunities for purposeful reading and writing are exploited. Progress is monitored and assessed by teachers who talk about books, who make and publish books of children's own writing, and who know children's books and how to organise and monitor the levels through which their reading can progress. Such positive and enjoyable ways of learning to read may need to be replicated for readers who are finding the start of reading a slow process or for older pupils who have difficulties.

THE LANGUAGE EXPERIENCE APPROACH TO READING

The use of Language Experience materials with beginning readers, known as the 'language arts' approach in America,[4] has had credence in the infant school since the early 1960s. The children's learning experiences were mediated by language in every possible way, talk leading into art work and into writing and children's written texts frequently being produced through the dictated words of an individual or a group. The Language Experience approach encouraged classroom teachers to create a 'language environment' which was practical and motivating. In an article describing both the historical background to this way of teaching reading and also the present practice Hall[5] concluded that: 'We have theoretical and research evidence that language experience learning is indeed effective.' In the National Curriculum for English for England and Wales welcome emphasis is made on the need for holistic approaches to reading and the encouragement of children as authors of their own books.

In order to identify the necessary conditions for reading we need a somewhat simplistic model of reading to show the important skills that readers need to develop on the way to becoming competent and fluent readers (see Figure 1).

All these skills are supported and developed when a child reads their own dictated text. The act of reading a longer and often more complex text develops reading 'muscles' and practises real reading in an authentic text situation whilst ensuring support and success in some of the most crucial areas of expectation and confirmation of letter/sound predictions.

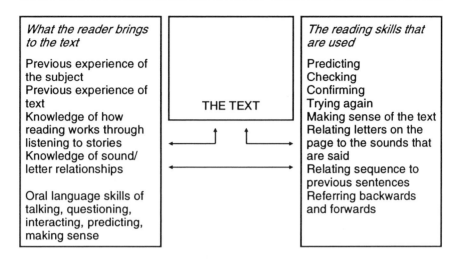

Figure 1 Model of reading and the skills involved

Why is this approach to reading important for children of all ages and abilities?

Attempts to meet the interest needs of older children often result in 'de-nurtured' materials which are apparently simple but which may put an unrealistic processing load on a learning reader. The content of such readers is often suspiciously suggesting that older poor readers need a diet of realistic but depressing dramatic happenings which supposedly reflect their own depressed backgrounds. Teachers know that between such social realism and the problems created by babyish books and remedial texts which will probably have already been tried, often in both infant and junior school, there is the anxious and increasingly passive reader for whom they are desperately trying to find a way into reading.

Children whose ability to write is limited, because of either their age or slow development of literacy skills, still appear to have internalised the conventions of written story – a knowledge of narrative genre which is shown from an early age.[6] Their dictated stories retain the fluency and some of the syntax of informal language whilst nevertheless edging towards the formality and patterns of written text.

There is increasing recognition by teachers of the importance of the language that children bring to school with them and the effectiveness of using that language to assist the development of reading, writing and oral skills in school. The work undertaken in my research, and subsequently in classrooms across the age range, is a justification of such recognition and both gives teachers practical ways of utilising the approach in the classroom and also validates the effectiveness and importance of using children's own stories as a way into learning to read and write effectively.

Infants learning to read and write

Children who are beginning to read and write use drawing as a way of symbolising meaning and communicating their ideas. Teachers often exploit drawing by asking children to talk about their drawing and then writing down what they say underneath.

There is considerable debate about the usefulness of children copying under the teacher's writing – without supervision incorrect handwriting motor skills can become a habit. It is, however, the process of talking about a drawing – indicating that there is a process of 'reading' the drawing which is taking place – and then the shared writing of the story of the drawing which replicates many of the composition and reading skills a child needs for independent reading of a written text. Using such told stories as a first story book for individual or class reading is a recognition of the child's own ideas and language. In some schools parents are involved in making such small books at home with their child and these become part of the home/school reading link.

There may be further parallels to the experience of writing when children are working with their drawings. Editing a drawing, going back to an original drawing and making changes which elaborate meaning, after questions and discussion with the teacher, shows the child that meaning is encoded in their drawings and that reflection and change allow meanings to be extended and communication made clearer.[7] This is exactly the process that is encouraged in young writers when we ask them to reflect on their writing and to talk about their writing with the teacher or with a writing partner. Using drawing as a planning agent before writing also allows many less fluent or competent writers to organise their thinking before they attempt to encode their ideas in words. Gary (10) drew the journey undertaken by the characters in his dictated story *The Three Silly Bears*. He used this drawing (Figure 2) as an aide memoire when he was dictating his story.

How dictated stories parallel this development of writing

In many infant classrooms young writers clearly understand the process of turning their own ideas and stories into books for themselves and for other children to read. They incorporate many 'book-like' features into their made books, indicating that they regard them as real books for real reading.

In what ways can dictated stories help older children who find reading and writing difficult to understand the processes of composing written text and enable them to learn to read more efficiently? We know that for

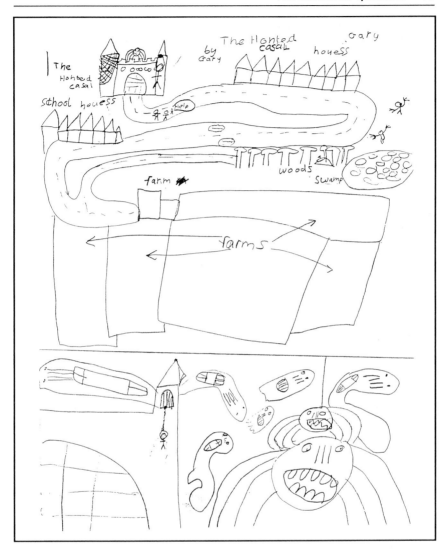

Figure 2 The journey of the characters in *The Three Silly Bears*

many less successful readers and writers there is little enthusiasm for the process; writing is slow and painful, reading laboured and uninteresting. As a result they do much less writing or reading than children who can already write and read. Their inexperience is not supported by increased practice and often the materials given to less experienced readers are artificially simplified by using short words and sentences, adding to the difficulties of motivation and interest. This makes understanding and meaning difficult if there are frequent pronouns and words that need to be referred a long way backwards or forwards in the text to find out what they mean.

In their own stories this does not happen if the task of performing the writing is taken over for them. It was Bereiter[8] who alerted teachers to the fact that if we could 'over-arch the performative side of writing for some children' they might surprise us by what they know about the process of composing written text. The slow and less confident writer is often limited to short words and simplistic ideas; they are not able to catch their ideas in writing and put them on the page because they are poor handwriters and spellers. When a competent writer takes over this performative part of the writing they are free to compose as they wish. Samantha (6) was unable to write anything on her own but the first paragraph of her dictated story shows many of the features of written text.

> *Princess Samantha, Prince Nicky they had a birthday party. It was their birthday today and they danced together all day.*
> *They had fun.*
> *Everybody had fun.*

Charles (11), a non-reader and writer, is able to compose an interesting text using complex sentence constructions to communicate his knowledge about fishing.

> *Fishing is exciting because you wonder what you can catch.*
> *In calm water you find carp.*
> *Where I go depends on how calm the water is; whether its a fast flowing river.*

Marie Clay[9] has written about the importance of treating reading and writing as reciprocal processes, both important in the teaching of beginning and less competent writers and readers. Allowing children to compose texts which they then use as their reading material makes clear to the child the reciprocity between reading and writing, whereas it sometimes seems that less confident children regard these as two unconnected and discrete activities.

An activity with a class of 11-year-olds in a school for children with moderate learning difficulties shows how children can be set free to write and to read. As a group they made a joint map and then composed a text which was written down and returned to them as a print-out which they were invited to change or add to as they wished. These children were perceived to be unable to write and their previous writing experience had been confined to exercises but their redrafts from the common text show how they had much to say if they were making changes rather than having to write an entire text on a blank page.

Three examples of changes to the first paragraph demonstrate the confidence they felt in their writing.

On Friday 13th October Mrs. South and Class 4 were going to Greece on a liner. The crew had food poisoning and Mrs. South took over. I was navigating. I made a mistake and we ended up hitting an iceberg.

One day Class 4 went on a liner but the Captain and the crew were food poisoned. So Mrs. South took over the driving and Neil was the navigator but Neil made a mistake and we ended up crashing into an iceberg.

Friday the 13th we went on a liner to Greece. But all the crew died of food poisoning. So Mrs. South become the helmsman and Gary become the navigater. But he steered us north instead of south but he made us hit an iceberg.

It is quite clear that these writers are experiencing, perhaps for the first time, a sense of control over their writing. Further developments included finding W. H. Smiths on the deserted island, roasting penguins over a bonfire, and finding a pink polar bear! The same sense of enjoyment in words and story can be seen as in John's tales of Bad Jim (see pp. 1–2). These children went on to use Front Page, a simple computer program, and showed even more clearly how much they really knew about written text (Figure 3).

The register of reporting is clear in this example – and the joke about the age of the headmaster again indicates writers finding a new sense of power in their writing.

This group approach to writing and rewriting and reading texts is considered in detail in Chapter 6.

Doubts and reservations

Teachers are sometimes concerned about responding too positively to writing down children's stories for them. They worry that such support will not result in independence in reading or writing and that children will not learn the important performative skills of writing if every important communication is scribed for them. These issues are dealt with in greater detail in later chapters but the main reservations are identified here and some indication of possible resolutions given.

Will children learn to read other kinds of texts? We know that there is concern about the limited kinds of texts which children write in primary school – particularly as secondary education demands a range of transactional writing in a variety of subject registers. Dictated texts can be in many genres – narrative, poetry, plays, instructions, information texts. Sometimes texts set out to be one thing or the other, sometimes different genres appear within the story setting. For example, Wayne (11) starts in narrative mode but includes specific instructional text:

One day I went out on my bike and I crashed I went back in and told my mum I had a crash. When I saw my bike it had a puncture. I didn't know how to fix

THE NEWS SPECIAL

25P

12.10.87.

STARVING CHILDREN RESCUED

9 PEOPLE SET OFF FROM THE ENDEAVOUR
AIRPORT.MRS.G WAS THE PILOT.THEY
CRASHED IN THE SEA.LUCKILY THEY HAD A
DINGHY.MICHELLE ,11,AND
MRS.G ,33,ROWED ALL THE WAY TO
THE ISLAND CALLED SKULL
ISLAND.ELIZABETH ,12,WANTED AN
AMUSMENT ARCADE.DANNY ,13,FOUND
A MAGNIFYING GLASS IN HIS POCKET.HE
WAS ABLE TO LIGHT A FIRE.STEPHEN
,13,HAD SAME STRING IN HIS
POCKET.HE MADE A FISING
ROD.CHRISTOPHER ,12,SAW A DEAD
BODY.VICTORIA ,11,WAS
CRYING.MR. S,95,SLEPT THROUGH ALL
THE EXCITMENT.

ISLAND PLANE CRASH

JOE'S WOOLLY JUMPERS

Figure 3 A Front Page report by a group of children

a puncture so my Dad taught me. This is how you do it.
Take the wheel off then use two spoons to take the tyre off. Get a bowl of water.
Find where the hole is by slipping the inner tube in the water and turning it.

It is quite clear here that Wayne is aware of the difference between telling a story and instruction. Kay (8) dictated an information text about the Vikings – the class topic. She could not read any of the project books on her own, but sharing them with a student and then dictating her own Viking information text helped her to understand the content and resulted in a useful book for others in the class to read (see Figure 38).

The Viking fighter had a heavy skirt of chain mails. He wore a cloak and a
brooch to keep it around him. He had a shield and a spear to fight with. He
wore a helmet with a bit over his nose to stop his nose getting hurt.

One possible solution to the issue of generalisation to printed text was pin-pointed by a non-professional helper and this is considered further in Chapter 2.

The analysis in detail of the composers' texts gives convincing evidence of non-readers' and non-writers' ability to use words and to construct and sequence texts.

The question of teaching children the performative skills of writing requires lengthy consideration as it involves understanding the process of writing and organising the classroom in such a way that the secretarial skills of handwriting, spelling and redrafting are supported and taught.[10] Less competent and enthusiastic writers often write most clearly and effectively when they are engaged in purposeful writing. Using a scribe to facilitate communication enables writers to practise composition skills even when they cannot write for themselves. There is evidence that such practice increases the motivation to write and also gives confidence and the experience of using extended text in an expressive way.

There are ways in which a child's dictated text can be used in order to lead them into learning the necessary secretarial skills of writing. We have already looked at the plan for writing made by Gary (10). His story, *The Three Silly Bears*, is amusing and inventive but also shows a surprisingly wide range of literary devices for a composer whose reading and writing ability was considered to be very poor.

He changes the story of *The Three Bears* to include an incident in which the bears hijack the Indian takeaway which Goldilocks has ordered by telephone. In her fury Goldilocks upsets the tables in the takeaway and goes off for a bus ride which leads her to the woods.

She got off the bus . . . and she smelled a curry smell.
"Curry! My curry and meatballs!" she said.
Looking down she saw big paw prints. She saw middle sized paw prints. She
saw tiny baby paw prints and meat balls rolling everywhere.

In the story of Baby Bear's first day at school the fun is orchestrated by using the same well-known devices:

He went to his class but he didn't like it. It was too big.
So they put him in the middle sized class but he didn't like it.
Then he went to cookery class and he showed them how to make porrige. The teachers said it was a good improvement.

How could this enthusiasm and commitment be extended to cover work on the very necessary skills of spelling and handwriting? Choosing the key words in Gary's writing – curry, bear, woods, scare – it was possible to make lists of words which looked alike although they didn't sound the same.

bear
ear
heard
earth
heart

These were then learned using look, cover, write, check as a technique. A mnemonic was made up to link the words together, they were practised, tested and then used in sentences. Gary's enthusiasm was considerable – they were after all his words – and he enjoyed the lighthearted game of learning to look and then to write.

The exploitation of dictated texts for the purposes of supporting other writing skills has to be done sensitively, often arising from the wish to spell a particular word. However, such extensions into learning to write can be undertaken by the scribe helper and can be a valuable support for a child learning to read and write.

Sharing reading opens up the classroom

The emphasis on enjoyment and meaningful reading has led to more open and relaxed attitudes towards reading in schools.[11] In this research the use of non-professional volunteers to act as scribes/listeners accords with contemporary concerns to make schools more open to outsiders and to involve parents more in reading and writing activities. Relationships formed between the child as composer/reader and the helper can lead into a variety of support work.

My own experience suggests that work which involves an on-going relationship with a child within which learning takes place is a satisfying experience for classroom helpers and results in long-term, high-quality commitment.

Links with important areas of learning to read and write

This brief look at the context for the research, and for the extended classroom use that has resulted from the research findings, indicates how much this approach to reading and writing has to offer teachers and children. Links with areas of the National Curriculum for English are given for those teachers who want to see how the reading context extends to current assessment in England and Wales. Important areas in a school's language policy can be clearly identified in the list below, and mapping the links with important areas of literacy should give teachers confidence to use this approach.

Reading

Learning to be an author   AT levels 2: 1, 2, 3, 4, 5
Understanding author/reader relationship   AT levels 2, 5
Independent reading behaviour   AT levels 2, 3
Developing all the reading strategies   AT levels 2: 1, 2, 3
Researching and reading for information needed   AT levels 2: 3, 4, 5

Writing

Planning   AT levels 3: 5
Sequencing   AT levels 3: 5
Creating characters   AT levels 3: 2, 4, 5
Developing plot   AT levels 3: 2, 4, 5
Cohesion   AT levels 3: 3, 4
Genre   AT levels 3, 5

Editing – reflecting and evaluating   AT levels 3, 4

Understanding difference between oral and written discourse   AT levels 3: 4, 5
Developing literary vocabulary   AT levels 3: 2, 3, 4, 5

Oracy

Talking in an interactive situation with an interested adult   AT levels 1: 1, 2
Learning to listen   AT levels 1: 1, 2, 3
Evaluating   AT levels 1, 7
Extended monologue   AT levels 1: 3, 4
Clarifying meaning   AT levels 1: 4, 5, 6
Developing vocabulary in interaction   AT levels 1: 3, 5, 6

The present, necessary concern about teaching all the aspects of reading, writing, talking and listening can be met through using a Language Experience approach to reading in a consistent and extensive way. When all the language involved in composing and reading a text is considered it shows that a surprisingly wide area of language learning is covered.

Chapter 2

The organisation and practicalities of using the Language Experience approach to learning to read

THE ROLE OF THE SCRIBE/LISTENER

Studies in language development[1] have shown the importance of the interactive relationship between adult and child in the development of language.[2] The way in which an adult supports a learner is sometimes called 'instructional scaffolding':[3] the teacher provides the structure so that composers can take on tasks which they would not yet be able to complete on their own. These kinds of structures underlie the task of scribing and listening. Scribes and composers working together are engaged on a common task for the clearly defined purpose of producing a printed text to read. The scribes make explicit the stages through which the composers will, eventually, internalise for themselves the process of writing. When a text is dictated, written down and then read the skills of reading are supported and encouraged by the interactions between the reader and the listener.

There is a triangular relationship between scribe/listener, composer/reader and dictated text which can exist in a great number of different settings and which covers within it all the important aspects of learning to read and write (Figure 4).

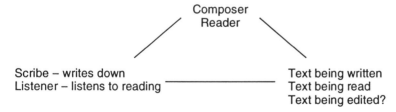

```
                    Composer
                     Reader

Scribe – writes down                    Text being written
Listener – listens to reading           Text being read
                                        Text being edited?
```

Figure 4 The composing/reading triangle

The composing and the reading of a dictated story are organised in a simple sequence:

dictate → print → return to child to read → continue dictation

In a classroom situation a routine can easily be set up in which the process and the organisation of the process are made clear to anyone working with a child. One such routine might be the one used with the helpers in the research sessions (see Appendix 1).

Different versions of this sequence of production could include:

1 *Typing directly onto a computer or typewriter* – helpful for an impatient child or a child with a very poor memory because the story can be read immediately.
2 *Scribe writing the first part of the story and the child then continuing* – bridges the gap between scribed and independent writing.
3 *Group story being scribed and then individuals invited to change or edit the original on individual print-outs* – introduces the idea of editing and gives a base for less confident writers to start from. If the story includes the name of someone in the group then they will all want to change that (see example on p. 13)!

What is not helpful is leaving a child with a tape recorder and asking them to tell a story and then writing it down for them. Transcribing from a tape is very time consuming but more importantly what is lost is the relationship underlying the triangle between the telling of the story and the intention of it being written down. *It is in the interaction between scribe and composer that the learning about writing and communicating seems to take place.*

Whose words are they anyway?

There is a difficulty for some teachers in accepting the way in which children tell their story and writing it down exactly as it is said. Often children use what is perceived to be 'bad grammar' when they dictate their story. For example, James (8) wrote:

The firemen comed

instead of

The firemen came

This is a problem of oral/written overlap in an inexperienced writer like James rather than a grammatical problem – some dialect interference is taking place. *At this point this is unlikely to matter.* Readers often correct such oral words or phrases when they come to read their story in print and then the story can be edited to more standard written English. What is important is that the composers' own words and phrases, words they can correctly predict and that are in their own language pattern, are encoded into print for them so that they can read them successfully. Changes to 'correct' English can be negotiated with the child for the purposes of public reading.

Interesting work has been done with second language learners where successive versions of a group story have been made with each new version tackling another aspect of the English usage. In this way the original story is not devalued or rejected as incorrect but is used as a basis for improving the use of English.[4]

How can this be done in the busy classroom?

Many different ways of producing dictated texts can be found if there is a conviction that the process is valuable and effective. Jack Gilliland started the Durham Printing Project which employed Youth Opportunity workers to professionally word process, illustrate and bind books for the Durham Remedial team . On a much smaller scale some primary schools have found neighbourhood secondary schools keen to undertake typing and printing as part of business courses.

The small-scale, less glossy but effective classroom computer has much to commend it, however. It allows for editing and changes to take place on original print-outs that are not yet proper books but are clearly printed texts. Texts can be stored on disk and easily accessed for new print-outs that incorporate changes. Extra copies can quickly be made. For group dictations every child can be given a print-out and then be asked to make their own changes.

The question most frequently asked is how can the busy teacher do this effectively – particularly if several children in the class would benefit from this kind of help? The stages at which all kinds of different help might be used are listed below.

Scribing/listening

    Teacher with individual
    Teacher with group
    Support teacher with individual
    Support teacher with group
    Welfare or auxiliary assistant with group
    Non-professional volunteer helpers

Typing out dictated texts

    Teacher – allows teacher to evaluate children's progress
    Support teacher – allows programmes for spelling, etc. to be derived
        from child's own work
    College or secondary school business course
    Volunteer helper/s

Making texts into books

> Writers themselves – illustrating the text as well
> Writers with helper
> Other children – class or club activity for printing, etc.
> Volunteer helpers

The most important element in the production of the text is the actual words and the interaction that creates the text. Texts themselves can be simply printed, stapled or sewn. Some children may not even want to illustrate them. Older writers and adults are often only interested in the printed text. In the relationship between helper and author, however, there is often a lot of positive and helpful work done when illustrations are considered and the format of the book is discussed and undertaken.

PRACTICALITIES AND POSSIBILITIES

Finding the time

The practical issue for many teachers who are convinced about the motivating and learning value in children reading their own texts is the sheer amount of time that such an undertaking demands. In secondary schools, and increasingly in primary schools, the claims of the curriculum exert pressure on how much time can be spent with individual learners. Many teachers like to make at least one book with a child or a group of children but feel that the consistent input necessary for pursuing this approach over a period of time is not possible. It is, however, the consistent and incremental nature of the activity, as well as the related activities of talk, research, reflection and evaluation, that seem to be crucial elements in changing children's attitudes and giving them confidence to read and write for themselves.

Help in the classroom

In order to find the time to help children make their own texts the classroom teacher may need the help of support teachers, teacher training students or untrained classroom helpers. All have valuable roles to play.

Many support teachers value working with the classroom teacher, with groups of children or with individuals. By acting as scribes they can produce books and other materials with children which support classroom topics and interests. Students in initial teacher training increasingly need to demonstrate classroom experience in many areas of their curriculum. Many valuable insights into children's reading have come through small group and individual projects undertaken by students where the production and reading of a dictated text has been the central enterprise between student and child.

Auxiliary help for statemented children is often given to teachers. Many of these helpers can be untrained and their valuable potential not fully exploited. They are in an excellent position to work with children in a long-term way. Making books with slow learning and Down's Syndrome children has been effective and there is considerable evidence to suggest that disturbed or unhappy children benefit from the chance to express themselves in a way that is precluded when they are not able to read and write for themselves. Using welfare assistance provided for children with emotional and behavioural difficulties can sometimes be most effective when it is related to achievement in basic skills. Finding 'the story of your life' through telling a fictionalised version of your life story may well be one of the most positive and effective pieces of class-room management of behaviour. It is an understanding that is rooted in effective and long-term learning of important skills.

The use of volunteer help in the classroom is a valuable asset in many primary classrooms. Such help is also available at secondary level if it is requested in the right way. There is evidence, however, that help that involves merely tidying or washing out paint pots, or even 'listening to reading' does tail off. It is important for helpers to have a sense of real engagement with children they are helping. Many of them have valuable interactional skills to offer. The long-term commitment and involvement of volunteer helpers in this project has been surprising and encouraging. It is here, however, that many teachers again raise concerns. Already reading seems high on the agenda for criticism and comment. How can they hand over part of that activity to a non-professional? On the other hand, teachers know that they cannot spend the time they need with the children who are having difficulties. It was with these important questions in mind that the training and organisation of non-professional helpers was undertaken in my research.

THE TRAINING AND ORGANISATION OF VOLUNTEER SCRIBES/LISTENERS

The use of competent writers, whether adult or peers, to write down children's dictated words in order to produce texts for reading is a well-established routine. It has credibility in all areas of literacy learning – particularly perhaps with very young learners and with older learners or adult illiterates. From my own informal experience I was certain that this was a useful way of helping many children to become readers but I could find no description of what it was that happened between helper and child or adult, nor any indication of what it was that the helper did that was most important in the process. There also remained the questions which teachers had asked about whether they could be confident that the prolonged use of non-professional helpers would be educationally beneficial to their pupils.

1 How would the volunteers understand their role as scribes and how could the task be organised?
2 Could the teachers know that the scribe was acting in a way consistent with their own practice?
3 What did the volunteers do in their capacity as scribes that facilitated the composing of the stories?
4 What other interactions took place between scribe and composer?

Additionally, many teachers might want to know where such volunteer helpers can be found.

The two phases of my research tried to answer these questions. Volunteers were identified and training given. A description of the training and training materials is given below to enable teachers to see how they could induct and train helpers in their classroom. It also gives a model for teachers, support teachers and auxiliaries using this particular approach to reading for the first time.

The materials were first devised to train a number of helpers, new to the classroom, for the first time. Teachers might want to use the materials individually or with a couple of already known helpers. In that case the actual format would be likely to be much less formalised but the points identified are still important and the use of the materials, and of the way of listening to children reading, would still need to be followed.

The initial meeting

All parents and interested people (including governors) in the school were invited to a meeting about 'Helping Children with their Reading'. Such a session would also be suitable for local SEN support teachers, welfare or auxiliary helpers, secondary, tertiary or initial teacher training students. On the initial invitation the main points were stressed:

1 The regular time commitment required (at least 45 minutes, with younger or SEN children needing shorter but more frequent sessions)
2 The nature of the involvement – a regular involvement with the same child on an on-going reading project
3 That some training would be given
4 That some writing was involved
5 That there would be an element of feedback and discussion with the teacher
6 That this was an interesting and important way in which they could help a child who had difficulties with reading.

These details gave volunteers some idea of what they were letting themselves in for. It also attracted some people who might otherwise have been less interested in 'helping' in the classroom.

At the initial meeting the volunteers were given a talk about reading and the way in which reading was taught. A short homemade video was shown in which the teacher was seen sharing reading in a relaxed way with a child with difficulties. What was made obvious was the shared talk and predictions that an adult and reader could have about a book.

On the second occasion, when some volunteers had already been trained, a video was made showing a volunteer working with a child, the child reading and talking about their dictated text and the volunteer talking about the experience of working with a child. The process of making a book was explained, and the books made by some children were shown and discussed. The way in which this helped children with severe difficulties was emphasised.

Volunteers were given an initial handout to take away. Those who were interested were asked back to a training session at a future date but no one was asked to commit themselves at this first occasion. There was a need for volunteers to type out the texts on the computer as an alternative to working with a child and it was hoped some people would feel able to help in this way.

The training session

The training session reemphasised the process of making a dictated text and dealt with the issue of listening to children reading. Certain points were emphasised:

1 The 'training' had been devised for non-professionals and was well researched and validated.
2 Feedback of an informal kind would be valued by the teacher.
3 The teacher would also give some feedback to the volunteer after two or three sessions. For this purpose it would be necessary to tape record the child reading to the volunteer.
4 The 'book' would be returned initially as a print-out and any alterations required could be made. Gradually a proper book would build up. Sometimes this would be a long story, sometimes it would be a collection of small stories. Information texts could also be included if wanted.
5 The importance of writing down the child's exact words was stressed.
6 The importance of the child's choice of content was also emphasised.

From the first phase of the research it had been found that any difficulties tended to relate to the vounteer's confidence and anxiety centred on the task. In the second phase the training dealt with these points and no difficulties were experienced. Volunteers needed feedback from the teacher to let them know that they were doing well. This was achieved by instituting a two-way diary in an exercise book in which the volunteers could write down anything they felt anxious about and the teacher could reply. In addition, the volunteers needed to be reassured that when the task of composing and reading didn't go well it was quite acceptable to do other things such as illustrations for the story, informal talk or going to the library to find out information. It was stressed that for some children the fact of having an interested adult to talk to was important in itself.

A room for working in was identified before this second training session. The room needed to be private, i.e. the child should not be in view or sight of other children and the noise level should be minimal. If possible it should have an electric socket for recording (unless a battery tape recorder is available), have a table and two chairs and not be too bleak – working in a storage space can be depressing!

A synopsis of the training (see Figures 5 and 6)

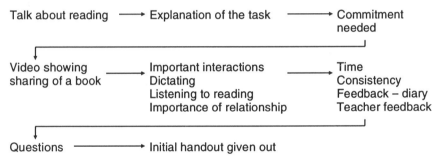

Figure 5 The process of the initial meeting

Materials were examined and discussed.
↓
Discussion dealt with questions raised by the volunteers.
↓
The *Helping with Reading* booklet was gone through in detail.
↓
The room where sessions would take place was shown.
↓
A possible timetable for helpers was given so that they could see where they might offer help.

Figure 6 Issues raised at the training meeting

It is obvious that such formal details as listed in Figures 5 and 6 might be more informally given if only one or two people are to be used as helpers. The precise use and understanding of the materials is, however, important. The long-term commitment of the helper is likely to be influenced most by their sense of confidence in what they are doing. For the child the validation of the helper by the teacher is of importance; for the teacher the knowledge that the helper is using an accepted and correct method when working with the child is essential.

Finally the confidential nature of the activity needs to be stressed. The teacher can explain the way in which the relationship will build between helper and child, and the importance of this relationship to the child. As with a teacher, exchanges between child and helper should be confidential. It may be felt necessary to formalise this in some kind of contract emphasising that information about the child should be talked about only with the teacher.

Partnerships between helper and child are a matter of intuition and experience for the teacher concerned, and the use of the feedback diary should prevent problems occurring. Whilst most partnerships work well, there are cases where the adult has a different agenda and is putting pressure on the child, e.g. one helper who wanted to 'teach' the child better handwriting and was found to be insisting on them writing. Adults who particularly request 'naughty' children don't always seem to enjoy the reality! Be prepared to change partners after the first few sessions if it is really necessary. In spite of having some very difficult children, I found that most relationships were positive and some were supportive and successful over a long term.

The materials (see Appendix 1 for full details)

How to be a scribe The initial flowchart was reinforced by further information.

How to start Some helpers found the first session difficult and giving details of how it might progress was found to be supportive.

The reading back The process is given and additionally details for changes. Teachers will note that the 'code' given relates to a redrafting code. If a different code is already used in the classroom then this should be substituted. It seems important to reinforce for children that redrafting your dictated story is the same cognitive process as redrafting your handwritten story.

The Help! *page* This was included after Phase One when the difficulties helpers found were identified.

Helping the transfer to ordinary books This addition to the materials was actually suggested by a helper. Teachers can decide when to use such instructions and whether to include them in the initial booklet.

The Listening to Reading booklet   This is based on Glynn et al.'s (1979) guide for parents helping children with reading difficulties. It is sometimes known as the 'Pause, Prompt, Praise' model. The cartoon version of the initial flowchart was found helpful in making clear to the helper what to do at each stage. It is in using this that feedback is important. I asked helpers to tape record the second time the child read back to them – explaining to the children that I wanted to listen to them reading. It was then possible to see whether the helpers were following the instructions. A result of listening to one pair was a note put into the diary to suggest that if the helper waited a little before helping it would benefit the reader.

The diary   This can be a simple exercise book, kept in the folder, in which the helper makes informal notes at the end of the session. This proved to be invaluable. Used initially as a way of giving support to the helpers it also became a way of assessing how the child was progressing as both reader and composer. It allowed informal comments to be fed back to the teacher and also let the helper raise difficulties which they might have been anxious about doing face to face or might have felt there wasn't time to ask the teacher about.

Initial sessions were reported:

> Talked at length about barn owls – he is very knowledgeable . . . . Went to the library to research owls – nest building. No luck but found excellent picture. Paddy, *Diary*

> We read all about the otter to get some background. Gill, *Diary*

and difficulties identified:

> Graham puzzled at first, needing to clarify 'telling a story' by questioning me closely. John, *Diary*

Checklist of materials

> Folder labelled with child's name, helper's name, day and time of session
> Biros, pencils
> Paper for scribing
> Drawing paper and felt tips or coloured pencils
> Instruction booklet
> *Listening to Reading* booklet
> Help sheet
> Scribe diary

Optional extras

> Picture books without words
> Joke books
> Another child's dictated story (as a model and for inspiration)

Working with a composer/reader

The first session was sometimes hard going and the adult required re-assurance that the establishment of relationship was more important than the enforced production of a dictated text.

Choosing a subject was a matter of long discussion with some partners, with others the child had a story they wanted to tell and they were ready to start immediately. Starting from an experience – holiday, outing – an interest such as fishing or a toy they particularly liked, the suggestion was made: "Shall we write this down?"

Using the materials: what the helpers did

In order to find out what it was that went on in a dictating or reading session tape recordings were made of all sessions over a period of time and as a result it was possible to specify what kind of interactions went on and what the role of the helper was in producing the final dictated text. Four categories of 'help' were identified[5] and they gave some useful insights into both the role of the helper and the process of dictating.

What went on between helper as scribe and child as composer

When the child was composing and the helper was taking on the role of scribe there were important aspects of writing that seemed to be made explicit by the questioning and the responses of the helpers.

Writing is a lonely occupation; decisions, alterations and structures must be created by the writer and it is only later, in conference with a teacher or peer, that inconsistencies or confusions become apparent. For novice writers struggling with handwriting and a limited or non-existent writing vocabulary, the ability to detach themselves from the performance of writing and become the reader reflecting on their own communication is an almost insuperable task. What happens in interaction with a scribe is that the process of reflection becomes integral with the process of articulating a story or ideas; helped by the scribe's clarifying questions and set free from the struggle with spelling and arm ache, the novice writers begin to be able to deal with the important aspects of learning to be a writer – planning and structuring a story, maintaining a se-quence, clarifying confusions and reflecting on necessary changes or improvements.

In planning, helpers assisted with organisation:

These things might help you to think of another story.
Shall I put some areas we might write about then you could think what would be the best sort of one?
We could do that – we could have two chapters.

and they reported on success. Gill noted that Mandy

Chose her title and story completely by herself today.

In the writing of the story the clarifying role of the scribe seems to be crucial to learning to develop a writing vocabulary and sustaining a story line:

It suddenly went Oooh!

dictates Corinna.

Can you think of a word to describe Ooooh!?

asks Tracey, the sixth former working with her

All of a sudden, looking out of the window when we was up, made my tummy tickle.

Corinna responds.

Sometimes there doesn't even need to be a question, just having a listener there is sufficient, as when Robert asks:

and the pals hid . . . hid . . . what do they call them?
Underneath a chalet . . . What do they call? Hut! Hut!
Underneath a hut

and his scribe Geraldine replies

Mmm. That sounds right to me.

Moving on a story is often difficult.[6] Paddy, in the diary, asks whether she might have been 'leading' Paul:

No difficulty in story-telling but I did have to push him into the final paragraph. He stopped at the end of the sentence and said "That's the end". I was very surprised and said, "Oh! Don't you want to do any more?" He said, "No. There isn't any more." I asked, "If you were reading a book and it finished there do you think it would be a good ending?" He said, "Not really . . . I know what . . . "

but it would seem exactly these kinds of probes and encouragements to move on or complete a chapter that developing writers need. In a similar vein John describes helping Graham:

I attempted to show him ways the story could continue when he suddenly began dictating . . .

The interaction taking place in the scribing situation was of a different kind to that of question and answer in the classroom. Here authority is usually invested in the teacher. In the dictating sessions scribes were interactive for the purposes of helping with organisation, memory probes and requests for clarification. The texts themselves remained very much the work of the composer. These developing writers easily became discouraged or wanted to give up – the response of the helpers provided the means for keeping the story going.

Editing

The request to scribes to ask the composers if they wanted to make changes to their text was introduced during the second phase. The suggested code was the same code that was being used for redrafting writing throughout the school. Additional materials were produced to support the editing stage. Where editing took place – often after several sessions – the reasons for editing were interesting because they often related to what goes into written text.

Jason's change is made to his delightful phrase:

come to his surprisement

a phrase generated in the excitement of trying to encompass meaning in words. However, on more sober reflection Jason changes this to the more conventional:

come to his surprise

because he says

"It's not really good to say surprisement."

Mandy, too, recognises on rereading, engaging with the text as a reader rather than as a composer, that oral story patterning, so effective when supported by intonation and gesture, may not be so appropriate for written text. So she changes:

looked and looked and looked

to one

looked

because

"I don't really want looked and looked and looked. I just want one looked."

Another composer, Paul, is encouraged to make a change which is factually different when his scribe asks him whether two birds (owls this time) would breed in the cage. This prompts Paul to change the direction of the story by changing:

more eggs in the cage

to

> *'I went up the mountain . . . and I saw another nest with six eggs in it'*

Here inexperienced writers seem to be engaging in a meaningful way with the possibilities of changing what they have written – a reflective stance towards writing which is needed when they begin to write for themselves. Changes may initially be very slight. Samantha (6) changed the title of her book from *Kirsty on Her Own* to *Kirsty Lives All on Her Own* when rereading her text, and then added to the ending,

> *At the end she had a parent.*

the fuller explanation

> *At the end she had a mum and dad. They came from Scotland.*

These changes often take place as a result of the feedback that helpers give to the composer:

> "That's coming really well."
> "Good isn't it when it's all put together?"

Robert makes an interesting response to the support of his choice of title:

> "That's a super title"

says his scribe:

> "That ain't a title that's a theme!"

he replies.

What went on between helper as listener and child as reader

These interactions will be considered more fully in Chapter 3 as they were an integral part of the reading development. It was evident that the same process of being 'alongside' the reader was an essential part of the successful relationship. There was an engagement with the text because of their joint part in the composition which perhaps removed the adult from the normal superior position of 'listening to reading' with a poor reader and rather substituted a real sharing relationship because each had an investment in the text that was being read. This seemed to be a particularly fruitful part of the reading activity. The tape recording of reading during the third session made it possible to give feedback where there were problems. A note in the diary to one helper, Gill, read:

> Lovely work Gill – you have got some very good responses from Lisa . . . let Lisa have a go at a word – read on beyond it even if it is wrong to see if she will correct it herself. If she doesn't just ask the question – does it make sense?

Cueing

The adults in the situation took on the kind of teacherly roles of recalling to task, remembering it was nearly dinner-time, deciding when enough chat had taken place and work should commence, etc. The relationship allowed for flexibility and there was little conflict in the situation. When working with young children who are very unmotivated or anxious it can sometimes be helpful to vary the task and to include friends in the story for a time. Mark (6) showed reluctance to engage in the task but was very happy to organise his friends into photographs to illustrate his story (of himself as the leader of the gang!). Once the photographs were there he had no difficulty in telling a story to go with them. No amount of 'cueing to task' would have been successful at this point and sometimes a negative response requires a change of emphasis or direction.

Personal interactions

Some children with difficulties seem to be helped as much or more by the opportunity to relate to an interested adult as by specific remedial reading help.[7] The chance to talk about themselves, to share ideas and discuss interests, seemed of crucial importance in this particular relationship. Some helpers were very supportive of their partners, and this friendship can be very important, particularly where children may be in conflict with their peers or unpopular in school. Some children have worries and fears that can be shared only with an adult they trust. Clive (14), who told the story of his life in a fictionalised form, in this way for the first time facing traumas, convinces that for some people, both adults and children, the opportunity to fictionalise, reflect and see objectivised their own fears, anxieties, loves and hates is of great importance. Ongoing work on the experience of disturbed children being given the opportunity to tell their stories suggests that there are interesting and important aspects of this activity still to be recorded.

Extensions of the scribing/listening role

Working to produce a finished text often included adding illustrations and researching books for further information. Use of illustrations included:

1 Child's drawings and diagrams
2 Photographs
3 Commercially produced pictures – including books without words
4 Maps
5 Carefully copied information pictures and diagrams
6 Pop-up formats
7 Flap books

In the focused interest and attention of the helper and the author there is enormous scope for originality and enthusiastic endeavour!

Kirsty (8) was a very anxious child, bright orally but with poor short-term memory and no apparent reading or writing competence. She didn't 'know' a story but loved the picture book *The Angel and the Soldier Boy*. Her story was a retelling of that book and was printed on clear overhead projector gells to overlay the pictures in the book.

Samantha (6) showed indications of influence from other stories where the repetition of:

> *She had to do all the cooking by herself.*
> *She had to do all the washing.*
> *She had to go to bed at the right time.*

echoes the repetitive language used in 'big books' and early readers.

A flap book made with a student used the child's only interest (which was insects) as a way into reading. Under every hiding place there was found to be an insect when the flap was lifted.

Lisa, an 11 year old in the research sample, wrote a story called *The Otter Family* with a volunteer. They found books in the library about otters to help with correct details about otters and how they live.

Corinna used photographs and pictures to illustrate her story of *My First Time in an Aeroplane*. She dictated her story to a sixth form helper and brought in brochures, tickets and all kinds of other items connected with her holiday. These were copied and used as illustrations.

Andrew, a bright but very reluctant reader, was helped when his mother typed out his long story for him. It was cut out and stuck into a book and then used for shared reading, talking and as the basis for further stories.

THE PROCESS OF COMPOSING A DICTATED STORY WITH A VOLUNTEER HELPER: CONCLUSIONS

The original questions raised by the use of volunteer helpers to act as scribes for the pupils' dictated stories related to both feasibility and effectiveness. The issue of what actually took place in the process of dictating was also considered to be of importance. The experience of training volunteers and then monitoring sessions through tape recording in Phase 1 made it possible to change certain aspects of the induction and support of the volunteers in Phase 2. The training package (see Appendix 1) is now able to be used effectively in the classroom. It has been used to train volunteer helpers, support teachers, students in teacher training courses and welfare assistants in special schools.

The analysis and categorising of the interactions which took place between volunteers and pupils indicated that volunteers do take on a scaffolding role, supporting and encouraging pupils in the initial and later stages of composing. Pupils were aware of the role of the scribe, adapting their pace of dictation to the need for writing and showing interest in the technical aspects of the writing down by the scribes. The volunteers proved able to control and organise the sessions.

The main role of the volunteers was that of helping the composers to make their story clear. By asking questions which demanded a clarification of ideas and organisation of the story they made explicit to the pupils the needs of the reader for clarity. They encouraged planning and modelled lists and ideas for plans. During the course of composing they asked questions which moved on the plot, encouraged more writing and helped with sequencing.

The inter-personal aspect of the relationship between volunteer and pupil proved to be of importance and a variety of interactions and activities took place which were not directly related to the dictating session. Relationships were formed in which pupils were confident enough to talk about problems on some occasions. The positive and confident way in which pupils and volunteers talked about the experience of composing, dictating and scribing the stories indicated that the relationship between the composer and the scribe was both effective and enjoyable. Informal experiences with a variety of children and adults have supported the evidence derived from the study. What is made evident, too, is the enjoyment and positive satisfaction experienced in this kind of activity by both volunteer and composer.

Chapter 3

Learning to read

When children experience difficulties in learning to read we can look for reasons within the child, within the teaching materials used and within the context in which the learning occurs. Each learner is an individual who brings different experiences to the task of learning to read, but all learners need interesting, motivating and 'real' reading materials which will help them to develop all the necessary skills of reading. All learners also require a positive and successful context in which to learn to be readers.

The use of a learner's own text as a resource for learning to read can be effective in all these ways. Unlike learning to talk, reading a text does not elicit any response, support or feedback from the text itself. One reason why 'listening to reading' has such a high profile in the primary school is probably because the teachers' responses to the reading allow feedback and support to occur.

The dictated story is suggested as a 'bridge' between oral language and written text. It can act as a bridge between the supported and active feedback experienced in talking and the formal, frozen quality of written text. We know from recent studies that the use of picture books with learners of all ages encourages talk about the story to be made explicit, sequences and outcomes to be predicted and conclusions both obvious and between the lines to be drawn. Using picture books is an effective way to make story text accessible to inexperienced readers. Dictated stories encourage this kind of support because they are highly predictable to the reader, who is also the author. Dictated stories take the process a step further towards the ordinary text because they also encourage inter- action at the level of the sentence by supporting grammatical cueing and at the level of words and letters within the words by supporting the relationship between sounds and letters, as well as being an intrinsically meaningful text to the reader. The role of the helper as they write down the story and listen to the reading involves the positive feedback which is an integral aspect of shared reading. This interaction between the helper and the reader also encourages independent reading and the reader's use of self-correction.

We know that the self-concept of the reader is closely bound up with their early success at reading and that relegation to remedial texts or repeated early stages of reading schemes can sometimes be counter productive because of the way such readers feel about themselves. The activity of producing a recognisable 'book' – whether a story or information book – does have status in the eyes of other children. The texts which are dictated often use ideas, plots and language in advance of that which the author could write for themselves; they are therefore able to show a level of understanding and competence in composition which can surprise their peers.

In my research the questions asked about learning to read related to three main areas of the readers' experience:

1 Attitudes towards reading and their perception of themselves as readers.
2 The ability to use all of the cueing strategies available to them.
3 Increasing independence as a reader shown through self-corrections and the intention to make sense of the text.

These areas are of importance to all readers of all ages. They indicate whether the reader is progressing towards confidence and competence, whether they are beginning to view themselves as readers and whether they have some understanding of the process they are involved in.

In the research project it was important to be able to show that even with older readers with severe difficulties there was a progress made towards reading competency using this approach. If this was so then teachers could confidently use dictated texts in the knowledge that they encouraged and supported real and significant changes in reading be-haviour. The evidence and examples in this chapter relate to the research sample groups but the results are generalisable to learners who are having difficulties whatever their age.

ATTITUDES TOWARDS READING AND SELF-PERCEPTION AS READERS

It is important for children to have confidence in their ability to read and this belief that they are readers plays an important part in reading pro-gress. When they are able to read a lengthy text which practises real reading skills they gain this confidence. The problem is that as children get older and still do not become readers they increasingly become less confident, less active and less positive in their approaches and more acutely aware of the differences between themselves and others in their peer group. A condition of 'learned helplessness' and passivity takes the place of the active, meaning seeking role of the successful reader.[1]

Interviews with young children to find out what they thought reading actually was, and what it was for, showed the possibility that confusion about the process of reading is one of the difficulties for some children.[2] Similar interviews with 11 year olds gave some indication of how they viewed reading and themselves as readers. They were clear about what reading was for – utilitarian and long-term purposes: jobs, reading letters and forms, finding out "what's on the telly". Only Andrew thought it was to do with "thinking" although two children saw it as being rehearsal: "they pronounce it out" and "they talk to people. They read some things, its words on paper" were some of their suggestions. These two also saw their problem with reading as being to do with factors outside themselves, Corinna because she "didn't use to go to school" and Robert who suggested he was like his dad "who couldn't and then he got glasses".

It is interesting that some of the children thought they could once read but then something happened and they couldn't do it anymore. All the children referred to feelings of anxiety: Mandy said it made her "go upset", Graham "felt silly" whilst Corinna "used to pretend to everyone that I could read" because "they used to take the mick out of you". Of the 11 children in the sample group all but one expressed anxiety about themselves as readers whilst seven of them were perceived by their teachers to have some kind of behaviour difficulty.

It is clear that if you are not a competent reader by the time you leave junior school you feel pretty bad about yourself. Alternative ways of enhancing status amongst the peer group lead some children into disruptive or disturbing behaviour. The importance of dealing positively with problems with learning to read early on is shown by the poor self-image of these older readers.

The role of the adult in the interaction during the reading of dictated stories is clearly a positive one. The kind of feedback which helpers gave during the reading of a story was always positive. The feedback related to both the reading itself and to the story: helpers told readers that they were "reading well", "improving", "better than last time". They also reflected on and often commented at length on the story itself. These dual positive reponses – you are improving your reading and the text you are reading is a good text – were important in the developing self-regard and confidence of the readers. In the interviews at the end of the eight week sessions all the readers commented on the improvement that they perceived in their reading. Three of them referred to books they had read at home such as *Charlie and the Chocolate Factory* and bird books. Dawn became an avid Judy Bloom reader and both Dawn and Lisa read to people in their family who were not able to read themselves. All felt that they had been helped and they were proud of their books which were read by other pupils in their class.

READING BEHAVIOUR – THE ABILITY TO USE ALL THE CUEING STRATEGIES

Teachers will be aware of children's strategies that they use for reading through their mis-cue analysis of reading undertaken in the course of normal classroom assessment. The analysis of mis-cues allows the teacher to set an agenda for learning, but this can be time consuming and many teachers feel diffident about their ability to construct remedial materials or to find appropriate books to encourage changes in reading behaviour.

Reading the extended text of a dictated story, often more demanding in its use of language and vocabulary than other available texts, allows the frequent practice of the necessary strategies. Although a helper listening to a child reading may not necessarily be aware of the underlying strategies that are being used, the teacher needs to feel confident that they are responding and listening to reading in a positive way that encourages the use of all the strategies and cueing systems. For this reason some simple kind of training programme for helpers is essential.

Glynn's model of listening to children reading[3] makes use of the three strategies readers need to use in order to be able to make sense of reading. This method of listening to reading, particularly when including feedback to the listener, is both useful and effective. It is sometimes called the Pause, Prompt, Praise model and was developed as a way of helping parents of children with reading difficulties to be involved in listening to their children reading. It is now widely used in shared reading situations by teachers and parents.

The three responses of Pause, Prompt and Praise echo the positive professional responses to reading given by a teacher. The Prompt questions encourage the reader to reflect on the strategies which they have not been using and encourage a wider use of all the strategies.

Listening to reading (full materials in Appendix 2)

Pause: Waiting for the reader to see whether they will change or self-correct their reading is important – some children seem to need time to be able to do this.

Prompt: Glynn *et al.* suggest that difficulties in the reading should invite different responses from the listener; the three prompts listed below model the cueing system.

1 *If the mistake doesn't make sense* then prompt with a clue about the meaning in the story
2 *If the mistake makes sense* prompt with a clue about the way the word looks

3 *If the reader doesn't say anything* ask them to read to the end of the sentence or go back to the beginning of the sentence again

These prompts encourage readers to use all the three strategies for reading:

1 *The grapho-phonemic strategy* – letter and sound correspondences
2 *The syntactical strategy* – the grammar of the sentence, the way the words go together
3 *The semantic strategy* – the way in which the text makes sense

Praise: Giving a positive response to the desired behaviour of correct reading or a self-correction after a prompt means that all responses are supportive and encouraging.

It is when all three of these strategies are used by readers that they can begin to feel confident. Children of all ages who are having difficulty in learning to read need to learn that all three strategies are necessary. The bridge text of the dictated story is an effective way of learning this.

Strategies for reading

A simple way of determining what is a reader's main strategy is to ask them the question "What do you do if you come to a word that you can't read?". Listening to them reading an unknown piece of text can check out whether they actually do what they say they do when they come to a difficult word.

My particular 11 year olds had only partial strategies. Some of them had relied too much on others – saying they would ask as their first strategy. Most produced some version of the grapho-phonemic approach using such phrases as "sound it out", "cut it up", "pronounce it out", "by the letters" and "spell it out". When asked to demonstrate this with the word 'flag' on a card several children could sound out the individual letters but not make it into a word. Dawn confidently said "f..l..a..g frog!". Here are readers over-generalising an important and useful strategy and using it in isolation from meaning or their innate sense of grammatical construction. In the same way younger children will sometimes make impulsive guesses which bear no relationship to the words and letters on the page.

How does reading your own story help?

For these older readers stuck on 'sounding out', dictating and reading their own story was important because, as the author of the text, they already knew what the sense of the text should be. The helper, drawing attention to whether their reading made sense, alerted them to the need to use the semantic cues within the text. The wild guessers were able to use phonics in the way that is most useful – to check out the exact word from the letters when they already had some idea what the word might be. Stories written in their own syntax and language pattern were easier to predict and easier to check for correctness because the reader was already familiar with the text from their composing and reflecting. In one coherent process all the strategies were practised as they read a meaningful text with understanding and increasing accuracy.

SELF-CORRECTION AND INDEPENDENCE IN READING

The growth of independence in reading is the first step to autonomy in learning. Behind the Language Experience approach is a philosophical understanding that learning to read is most effective when learners use their own linguistic resources in a supportive and enabling situation. Some models of teaching reading may de-skill learners and make them feel that all the linguistic resources for reading have to be learned in some way. Older poor readers seem to be caught in a double bind: they are not able to read independently the texts they are given, and reading can be a 'showing up' situation if teachers try to help with easy texts. They therefore do less and less of the task at which they are failing. Difficult or disruptive behaviour is one way of diverting attention away from their difficulties with reading.

After so many years of failure and confusion it was perhaps inevitable that the pupils I worked with should have acquired learned helplessness. In the research sessions these readers had the attention of an interested adult able to scaffold the task for them. They made use of their own language by composing texts using their own words and by reading them in a situation which was supportive and unthreatening. As they found they could read and understand the texts they had created their confidence increased and so did their ability to be aware that they had made a mistake and to correct it.

The use of self-correction

Readers who do not have a range of strategies available for use in their reading tend to de-code individual words, or parts of words, without regard to meaning *within* the sentence, let alone *beyond* the sentence. They will suggest words that they know from their oral language cannot follow in grammatical sequence. A reader can begin to be autonomous only when they have an engagement in the overall meaning making, which is the central activity of reading a text. Mismatches between words that are read and the sense that they make cause readers to pause and reflect and then to have another go at the difficult word. This kind of activity – predicting, confirming or rejecting – is central to reading efficiency. If poor readers begin to self-correct they are practising the kind of reading behaviour which will allow them eventually to become independent readers.[4]

WHAT IMPLICATIONS ARE THERE FOR THE CLASSROOM TEACHER FROM THESE RESEARCH FINDINGS?

As a result of a detailed mis-cue analysis of each reader's reading of their own dictated stories over eight sessions evidence supports the value of using dictated stories as reading texts. There were changes in the way in which pupils approached difficulties in reading – demonstrated by both their mis-cues and the indication that they were using the range of graphophonemic, syntactic and semantic strategies and by the way in which they talked about how they tackled difficulties when reading at a later interview. The readers did not seem to be able to articulate the changes which had taken place in their reading strategies but there was evidence that they were using all three cueing strategies by the end of the research in both phases. The increase in self-correction, often related to mistakes which did not make sense in the text, indicated an intention to make sense of the story. Towards the end of the eight sessions mis-cues were often related to substitutions which occurred as the reading became faster and more fluent, and they tended to be substitutions which did not alter the sense of the story.[5]

The final interviews with the pupils showed that they regarded the volunteers as having played a part in their increased confidence in themselves as readers.

Jason says:

"Well I got on with my reading quite a lot really with Peta."

Graham says of an effective strategy:

"John taught me that."

For children who may have partial or incorrect views of how reading works, reading their own dictated story encourages the use of all three cueing strategies and allows complete texts to be tackled. Meaning is integral to the story – they know what the text should say – so self-correction is encouraged.

As readers become more successful at the task of reading they read more fluently and confidently and thus they perceive themselves to be better readers. If helpers are trained to listen to reading they can support the reader, feedback positive and helpful evaluations of reading to them, and prompt them with questions that help them to reflect on the meaning and the words in the text.

GENERALISING TO OTHER TEXTS

One solution to the problem of generalising to other printed texts was suggested by Robert's helper. She and Robert wrote some information texts in which they included descriptive or informative material taken from a printed book. The flow between the dictated text and the formality of the printed material is helped by the shortness of the initial inserts. Interest in the subject also helped with the transition.

> My Dad's got two cars; a Range Rover and an Avenger – that's me mum's – its orange.
> The Talbot Avenger is a two-door or four-door saloon or estate car with 1.3 or 1.6 litre engine. First introduced over ten years ago, but there are still plenty on the road.

Dean, described later in Chapter 6, generalised from his dictated text when a passage in which he is seen to be important and competent was written into his text for him.
Dean dictated:

> One day Mr. Street bought a surfing board.
> He did not know nothing about surfing.
> He went out to the sea.

The teacher added for him:

> Dean said he would show him.
> Dean got a board and paddled far out into the waves.
> The waves were even bigger now.
> An enormous wave rose high up into the air.
> Dean stood up on the board.
> He felt the shudder of the water under the board. He stood up and raised his arms.
> With a great rush the wave went high into the air.
> Dean stood up high above the water and the surf board rose up on the wave.
> Dean was thirty feet above the water.
> Then the wave broke.
> The surf was thundering in onto the shore. Dean came in on his surf board.
> Everyone on the beach cheered and clapped.
> Dean sat down on the beach.
> "That's how its done!" he said.

The insertion was requested by Dean because he said he didn't know enough about surfing to be able to write an exciting chapter. Putting Dean into the central position intrigued him and helped him to want to read on without too much anxiety. Discovering that he had been able to read a page of text which he had not dictated convinced him that he was able to read.

There are some children whose difficulties seem to be intractable and they may need special support and help. In Chapter 6 further details are given of children with severe difficulties. Jeffrey, who could not remember how to write his name, was referred to a dyslexia clinic and had the greatest difficulty with reading although he was a good oral communicator. His dictated story of a school trip was read over and over again and words were learned that occurred in the text.

Alan is taking a cooker
and David is taking a gas lamp.
We will all be saving up for food.
Miles is going to bring his rubber dinghy.
We might kick Miles out of the tent every night
or sling someone in the river!

There are cross-curricular implications if the importance of these dictated bridge texts is accepted. The creation of dictated texts to support topic work and to support other areas of the curriculum will result in 'books' for the classroom library which are the product of shared research in information books and which are able to be read by their author, and by others in the class. In this way books that are highly motivating and readable will support readers in many aspects of classroom learning.

CONCLUSION

Learning to read using your own dictated story is an effective and successful experience for children who have often experienced failure over many years. The fact that this is a different kind of activity, enhancing status and having validity in the eyes of peers, seems to be encouraging to children lacking in confidence. They feel that they are progressing in reading. It may be that there are residual reading skills, learned over many years, which are available to learners but that are masked by their repeated fear of failing and their difficulties. When a reader is helped to compose their own reading book, and when their reading is listened to in a sympathetic and positive way by a helper who is closely involved in the whole enterprise, the whole range of reading strategies begin to be practised by the reader. The central purpose of reading – to gain understanding, information and pleasure from a meaningful piece of writing – is supported in the Language Experience approach.

Chapter 4

Learning the language of writing

The evidence that dictated stories work as reading texts for children with difficulties began to raise fascinating questions about the text itself. If these dictated stories were a serious form of text for the induction and engagement of young and inexperienced learners then what was the language and structure of a dictated text like?

We know that texts differ from child to child, that often they show idiosyncratic language, ideas and interests and that they are close to the child's own oral language. On the other hand, even very young children seem to understand that in dictating a story to someone who writes it down they are in some way engaging with writing rather than talking. Composers are seen to search for the 'right' word, to try to describe events clearly even when that requires rather cumbersome language. Jason wrote about an eagle killing a fox to provide food for the baby eagles:

> *He started eating it and gave some of it to his babies, but that didn't mean just to go up and down to the fox and get their two children's food but they had to still go out and get their worms and insects and things . . .*

Jason struggles here to be explicit and convey his meaning to the reader – a struggle he would not need to undertake in a conversation supported by gesture, intonation and shared meanings.

Evidence about the discourse, the kind of language that is in a dictated story, gives an insight into the linguistic resources of children who are not competent writers as well as validating the dictated text as a proper vehicle for learning to read by showing that it has a demanding complexity like a formal written text. Writing can be seen as a continuum in which oral discourse in the form of gossip is at one end and poetry and pure logic is at the other. It should be possible to see where, on this continuum, the dictated story should lie. At first it seems to be a simple case of deciding where talk ends and writing begins, and finding the place there for the bridge text of the dictated story. This, however, raises the question of whether dictated stories are just 'talk written down'[1] or whether there are linguistic features present that are closer to writing.

The processes of writing include writing and revising, reflecting and conferencing. These processes cross over the oral/written divide. The audience for the dictated story is both implicit and explicit; on the one hand the scribe gives an immediate 'response', allowing the composer to judge whether their message is getting through, on the other the composers know that they themselves will be coming to their story as a reader in the next session.

American sociolinguists[2] have looked at the way in which speaking and writing overlap. This notion of overlap – some writing, like letters, being more like speaking, some speaking, like lectures, being more like writing – has been particularly useful and the concept of written 'spokenness' and spoken 'written-ness' has created a space in which to address the nature and function of the dictated story. Literary stories are perhaps closest to talk because of the need for the author to engage the reader in a close exchange of empathy and shared context. The understanding of the importance of story as a means of interpreting and expanding on one's own life experiences presupposes such an engagement between author and reader.

A view of the writing continuum is therefore suggested in which the divide between oral and written discourse shows an overlap in which certain kinds of writing and talking have common features with dictated stories, containing elements closer to writing than to talking (Figure 7).

What is important about written features that are present in dictated stories is that they indicate that pupils who cannot reach an effective performative level of writing for themselves do, nevertheless, have an understanding of the demands made in writing. The evidence that written features are contained in dictated stories demonstrates the developmental benefits of using the approach with younger writers and the importance of bridge texts for older poor readers and writers because they allow them to develop some aspects of their potential writing ability.

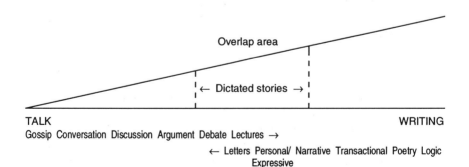

Figure 7 The place of the dictated story on the writing continuum

THE RELATIONSHIP BETWEEN THE DICTATED STORY AND ASPECTS OF WRITING (DEFINED IN THE NATIONAL CURRICULUM FOR ENGLISH)

Authorial		Dictated Story		Secretarial
Planning	←	Planned	→	Handwriting
Composing	←	Dictated to scribe	→	Spelling
Conferencing	←	Clarified in interaction with scribe	→	Punctuation
Redrafted	←	Edited sometimes	→	Grammar
Take the reader's role	←	Be the reader of the text	→	Presentation for audience

Figure 8 The relationship between the dictated story and aspects of writing

Aspects of knowledge about language

Understanding of the reader/writer relationship
Knowledge of genre
Cohesion
Differences between oral and written discourse
Standard English – in written form

The stories written in the research project were analysed and then described in terms of

1 the sentences used in dictated stories,
2 the vocabulary used in dictated stories and
3 the focus of the story – how the writer engages the reader

in order to gain evidence for the validity of the claim that dictated texts contain important elements of writing and are a good bridge text for novice writers of all ages.

The question of the sentence: differences between talking and writing

The difference between speaking and writing is apparent in the difference between the told 'on the fly' bursts of talk with their lack of sequencing, their 'co-operative overlapping' and limited use of vocabulary, and the complete sentences of the dictated stories.[3] In talk there are often breaks, repetitions and use of language carrying no meaning, e.g. "anyway", "umm", which are used in conversation as a means of giving the talker time to sequence or marshal thoughts and ideas, or to recall the thread of the discourse. In contrast to the fragmented and tentative utterances of speakers the composers dictated their stories in such a way that the scribes recognised that they were in complete sentences and they scribed in punctuation to this effect.

The conjoining of sentences in talk and writing

Chafe identifies conjoined sentences, usually conjoined with 'and', as a characteristic property of speaking. Novice writers too tend to conjoin rather than to subordinate or embed clauses in their sentences.[4] It would be expected that in dictating, conjoined sentences would be prevalent, although experience of composing and writing might encourage composers to use sentences that were longer and that contained some embedded or subordinated phrases and clauses.

It has been suggested that growth in the complexity of sentence production is an indication of syntactic maturity.[5] Not all increases in length may, however, contribute to clarity of communication. Analysis of sentences showed that increase in complexity did not necessarily indicate an increasing ability to put ideas and happenings down in a convincing and clearer way.

Andrew wrote:

A man pushed a woman into the road and her husband killed him.

and Robert

And the German hospital vehicle had put the injured in the back of the hospital vehicle and the prison what they were going to – it was called Colditz – it had big walls and gas chambers.

Both these sentences show the difficulties that immature writers can have with handling a sequence of events whilst retaining a hold of syntactic construction within the sentence unit. However, Darren's

He drives onto the beach with his mate. His mate gets stuck in a hole. Luckily Sam had a rope.

has the short, rather jerky quality of a beginning writer's written sentences compared to the later fluency of

I was going snorkelling but everybody else sat on the beach because the water was too cold.

The experience of composing and reading their own stories enables some composers to use words in a more complex way, and to maintain the thread of their story by beginning to embed and subordinate parts of their sentence; but the complexity and the degree to which sentences are embedded was not necessarily an indication of an ability to use words meaningfully and to keep the text hanging together. In the case of Andrew and Jason their gradual ability to handle ideas and sequences resulted in simpler but more meaningful sentences.[6] The structure of the sentence and the sentence complexity are not correlated and we should not expect composers necessarily to move from simple structure to more complex structures. Sometimes the reverse will be true as they gain confidence in expression and in handling the constraints of expressing what they want to say. One of the ways in which a sense of tension, or of events rapidly succeeding each other, can be created is by using short, simple sentences.[7] Dawn, in Chapter 6, used such simple sentences to describe a rapid succession of exciting events:

> *We opened the door and jumped out. I pulled the string. The parachute opened.*

Another aspect of learning to write and to use language is that children may appear to make more mistakes, both in talking and in writing, when they are struggling to synthesise new structures and vocabulary into their language use. Teachers need to be aware of this so that they can see that examples of confused or incorrectly used language may be indications of progress rather than laziness or lack of attention.

No real conclusion can be drawn from the complexity of sentences. However, sentences which are dictated, although produced in the oral mode, have more of the features of written sentences than of conversation. Even when writing dialogue the composers used complete sentences; some of these sentences were complex and contained subordinated clauses. The sentences in a dictated text are likely to be as complex or more complex than those in reading materials matched to the readers' reading ability and they certainly use and practise sentence construction through dictating at a level far beyond the composers' capabilities when they are writing for themselves.

Conjoining and coordinating of sentences in dictated stories

As children learn to extend their range of communicative functions they do not replace old forms but old and new forms coexist together. An increasing understanding of the range of linguistic functions available for use in both speech and writing grows alongside an understanding of the purposes and content of communication. In the composing of dictated stories some of the constraints of speaking 'on the fly' are apparent but the planning role encouraged by the scribes seems to have an effect on the composers' ability to plan their discourse. The planning and the experience of reading their own compositions and seeing them in written form may be what encourages a shift away from conjoining towards the use of dependent clauses using other conjunctions.

The conjoining words used by the composers were in two categories: simple conjoining words such as 'and', 'then', 'and then' and 'and so', and the more complex conjoining words 'so', 'but' and 'because'. When composing a dictated story many of the coordinating structures used are similar to those that apply in speech. In particular 'and' and 'then' are used as conjoining words for simple predications. The composers 'move on' the action of the story by stringing on the next event in the same way as early stories told by children 'chain' the series of events. It would appear that the experience of using language for written purposes does allow more planning and organisation to take place and that this shows in the increased use of the conjunctions 'so', 'but' and 'because' in the later chapters in the composers' stories. Other subordinating conjunctions were apparent. Many of the constructions used seem to be an attempt to use subordination without necessarily having the resource of the correct conjunction available. Subordinating structures such as 'what . . . they was going to . . .', 'what was near', 'after that', 'that they come back' and 'to find' would seem to indicate a struggle to organise subordinated sentences that retain some of the features of oral discourse rather than the formalised conjunctions of writing. Other conjunctions used by the composers fell into a time or sequencing function: 'after', 'when' and 'as' often occurring at the beginning of the sentence with the subject clause following on. For example:

When I was ten we went on holiday in Devon.

When we got there we had to walk down an alley.

After I had my dinner I showed my Dad . . .

These conjunctions, which indicate a sequence of time, might well be being used by the composers as markers to help them organise and sequence their story. The use of 'that', 'what' and 'to', as in 'to see', 'to go', is usually an example of a colloquial or speaking-like conjunction.

Robert writes:

what was in ruins
what they landed in
what was used

Paul:

I was happy that they come back.

Graham

. . . to tell them that

Written constructions would be more likely to be:

which was in ruins
where they landed
I was happy because they came back
in order to tell them that

There is evidence here that composers are attempting to do more than conjoin sentences in a simple way, as they might do in talk or in early writing. These are attempts to use writerly-like constructions because composers know that written text, even when you are dictating it, is substantially different from talk.

The vocabulary of the dictated story: words for talking, words for writing

The words in a dictated story are placed in the overlapping area between talking and writing. The story is generated in the spoken mode with the intention of becoming a written text although the constraints of talking to some extent apply. On the other hand, the intention of producing a written text, and the freedom from the need to attend to the demands of hand writing and spelling, allow the composer of a dictated story the opportunity to view the text, whilst composing, as a writer might reflect on a piece of writing in progress. The product of the spoken composing is there in tangible form for review and rehearsal. The scribes provide an audience who will demand clarification, causing the composers to re-think or to search for more suitable or apposite words for their purposes. The dictated texts produced in this oral context have some of the vocabulary and literary qualities of written text.

Literary words and phrases

The use of a 'literary' vocabulary to create effect is in part the result of involvement or audience awareness. A stylistic device such as 'literary word or phrase' is difficult to define but words or phrases considered unlikely to have been used in the speech of the composers but likely to occur in written language were identified as being in this category.

Robert used descriptive verbs to express what he was trying to say:

flew open
dropped out of the sky
slowly opened with a creak
started to collapse

he also chose his words with care:

heavy arms
mansion
in ruins

Where colloquialisms were used they mainly fell into the dialect form of incorrect use of words:

> *We never found Robert* (Graham)
> *should of* (Lisa)
> *patrol what was near* (Robert)
> *After it was lunchtime* (Wayne)
> *We come up on . . .* (Corinna)

Words or phrases such as these were common in the spoken language of all the composers. They also used slang or commonly used words or phrases such as:

> *Okay*
> *nicked*
> *she went bonkers*
> *loads*
> *massive*

but this was often in the context of conversation.

Andrew shows an awareness of acceptability of some kinds of language when he makes the decision to put in a? on two occasions – the equivalent of the BBC bleep.

> *Spider kicked him in the ?*
> *Shut up you old ?*

He was unlikely to show such constraint in his talk and therefore might have been indicating an awareness of the public and permanent nature of writing, in particular of school writing, where certain words are not acceptable.

The most frequently used colloquialism in these stories was 'nick' or 'nicked' which was used on ten occasions. It is also used as a noun ('the nick') twice in place of the word police station. Other common words were:

> *mucking about (3)*
> *kids (3)*
> *quid (1)*
> *bloke (4)*
> *mates (10)*
> *loads (4)*

There were occasions on which composers, using colloquial language, on a second occasion showed that they knew the more formal version which was more likely to occur in writing. For example, Graham dictated:

> *Please take sorry*

and the answer was:

O.K. I'll take an apology.

Later he put:

I smacked him in the mouth.

again followed by

to hit him in the mouth again.

It would seem that poor readers and writers, composing using a scribe, are able to use literary as well as colloquial language. It should not always be assumed that a colloquial phrase or an obviously oral construction is there because they have no other resource to use. Sometimes they do know more formal ways of expressing what they want to say. The lively nature of some of the stories, fast moving and even racy in expression (one is reminded of Justine's story quoted in the Introduction), depend to some extent on some of the oral aspects of language to create a mood of the events. Mandy's 'smack up together' and 'mad of sweets' have an immediate and individual appeal which might disappear when more formal and stylised aspects of writing vocabulary are internalised.

An interesting comparison of the composers' perceptions of the differences between spoken and written discourse is available in an inter-textual form. All but one of the composers used dialogue at some point in their story. Generally colloquialisms are seen to be part of spoken language, although written texts such as letters often have a high incidence of colloquial vocabulary in them. Other properties of spoken rather than written language are what we often term 'bad grammar' or 'sloppy speech'. Loose pronominals, unreferenced items, verbs and their antecedents not agreeing and contractions such as 'I'll' or 'they're' are more likely to occur in spoken than in written language.[8] The old lady who owned the pub in Mandy's *Painting Ghost* uses a number of colloquialisms in dialogue

I'm not stopping you
I'm popping out
run me up the town

which contributed to the liveliness of the text and the development of the character in the story.

Dawn, using dialogue a good deal, used many colloquialisms. Talking to his dog Nuisance, Crumple exclaimed:

You stupid dog
Bad doggy!
get off me
I've had a hard day

The composers reflected some of the features which are common to oral speech in their dictated dialogue, using, for example, a considerable number of contractions and colloquial language, particularly interactive colloquialisms such as 'OK'. The dictated dialogue, although composed in an oral mode, was seen to be part of the written text. Contractions and colloquialisms appeared to be used as a way of differentiating dialogue from the main text of the story.

Is that bad grammar then?

The talk of all the children in the sample group showed patterns of verb and antecedent inconsistencies. These were considered to be more likely to be dialect interference rather than an indication of lack of knowledge of how number and tense should go together in the use of verbs. This inconsistency is a feature of oral discourse which is unlikely to appear in writing. The most common types of inconsistency have already been noted as colloquialisms in the text. Most common were 'they was' and 'they done' with 'come' and 'comed' also in frequent use. In New Town dialect these are common forms to hear.[9]

It does not seem that such inconsistencies were being used in a conscious way to differentiate speech from prose, but rather that they are forms of discourse which are so familiar to the composers that they have not yet realised that they are inappropriate for written text.

The focus of the story: involvement of the reader

In talk the obvious face-to-face nature of involvement and response with the audience means that there are certain "you know", "don't you think" type interactions in the discourse. In narrative this is an important area where involvement is an element of writing as well as speaking.

Speakers share a context which they mediate non-verbally, in order to clarify or emphasise the content of their conversation. Unreferenced items can be clarified if necessary at the listener's request but talk can remain 'minimally explicit' because the speaker often shares a context with the listener. Conversation is often insignificant but carries important inter-personal meta-messages. Writing, however, is de-contextualised: confusion on the part of the reader has to be anticipated and a shared context cannot be assumed. Areas which cross the oral/written divide would include love letters or notes which show person-focused involvement in the written mode, and instructive television or radio programmes which are message focused in the oral mode. As we have already noted, the dictated story shows composers using talk for the purposes of producing written text.

Speakers achieve cohesion in their discourse by intonation and gesture.

In writing, cohesion must be tackled as part of the writing itself. Some of the cohesive devices used in speaking can be found in writing, specific statements which 'nudge' the reader to indicate that an inter-personal message is being conveyed. In writing, words must be chosen carefully to give the exact required effect and connotation in order to facilitate the communication of feelings and creation of context between author and reader.[10]

The demand for written explicitness in their stories was achieved by scribes helping the composers by interpreting their non-verbal cues in a face-to-face situation so that the composers developed some of the strategies which help to involve a reader in a story. In these told stories, composed with the intention of becoming a written story, are literary elements close to those elements in conversation which retain the listener's interest and empathic response.

Examples of ways in which the composers used language to involve the reader

Repetition was used by the composers, whether to give breathing and sequencing time or as a deliberate device it was difficult to determine in some cases.

Darren's

Sammy's mate made Sammy's buggy tip over and Sammy was upset.

and Graham's

Then Graham's cousin came. Then Robert's cousin came . . . there was a fight with Graham's cousin and Robert's cousin and then Graham's cousin won the fight.

seemed to be more a way for the composer to organise the complexity of relationships and characters than an intentional device to create effect. However, there were uses of repetition, particularly of initial letters or sounds, which seemed to intend just such an effect on the reader:

it made my tummy tickle
you had better beware
Pepee, Sweep and Neepee

Some composers used parallel constructions to create a particular feeling and atmosphere. Darren used

splashing around . . . and stirring up

in juxtaposition. In the same way Andrew used:

shouting and singing and banging

as a device to create tension within the story.

Corinna's repetitions appear to be deliberate:

then the baby jumped on his dad and cuddled him then he jumped on his mum and cuddled her and then they all had a cuddle together

and in the same sequence she used the words

lumpy and bumpy

which went beyond mere description and seemed to be consciously rhythmic and parallel in construction. Graham uses the compelling rhythm of

he was dead floating around and around and around.

Dawn created an effect with the sentence:

threw it so far you could not see it in the air . . . ran so far you could not see him.

Jason, in his intense desire to express what he felt, invented a word to fit what he wanted to say:[11]

come to his surprisement, opened his wings and glided gently down to the ground.

Some of the composers appeared to be more conscious of the effect that words in certain order and juxtaposition can have and the rhythms that they can create in order to engage the reader.

Lisa composed:

Blonk! Blonk! Blonk! went the otters in the water
Splash! Splash! Splash! at the bottom on the weir

and she used such phrases as:

all day and all night

and

The Killer Whale has a very strong tail

Dawn showed a command of rhetorical language with:

You'll have seven days to stay here but if you're not gone in seven days you'll be burned on the bonfire.
I will give you seven apples.
You will eat one every day.
So when the seventh apple comes you will say Goodbye to the world.

– words which have a biblical ring to them, as have Jason's

The end and a new life had just begun.

Even Wayne and Graham, generally far more prosaic in their descriptions, rose to the excitement of their specialist knowledge with Wayne's

He's on the 1 to 9. I'll be on the 1 to 4.

and Graham's

the Looping Star, the big Bumper cars, the Mary Rose, the Big Wheel, the Roller Coaster and the Water Chute.

Paul, whose final poem was a delicate invocation of 'owl-ness', shows that he knows how to use language to engage his reader:

Push down with your hand
In the feathers
Fluffy head, small skull.

Big head,
Big body,
Big feet, sharp claws.

Swooping down for its prey.
Got it!
Go back home.

although much of his story is information focused, sharing his knowledge about owls and their rearing.

The 'nudges'[12] in spoken language, which can be written in involvement-focused discourse, can be found in these dictated stories. It is difficult to determine whether they started as asides to the scribe which the scribes then decided to lexicalise or whether they were truly reader focused. Many of these 'nudges' come about as a desire to explain something which was not apparent in the text. Robert amplified his description of place with

It was called Colditz

and of the pass card system with

A pass card is a round circle with an eagle on it

Wayne explained a 'backy':

that's when you sit on the back of the seat of someone else's bike

Lisa tried to bridge the gap of understanding between the reader and her otters by an aside:

to us it looked like they was slipping

when describing the otters' skating escapade. She also explained:

the other three laughed in their own language

to remind the reader that the Safari Park incidents were filtered to them through the otters' experiences.

A second type of 'nudge' would seem to be a truth statement:

this is a true story
we have still got it now

Wayne in his initial chapter told the reader:

this is how you do it

before giving instructions about mending a puncture.

A third type of aside would seem something like 'in a humorous vein'. They consist of little asides aimed at involving the reader in a shared joke or the complicity of shared knowledge.

Dawn's

Can you guess who it was? It was NUISANCE!

and

Anyway my teeth look quite nice after eating those seven apples

were devices which engaged the reader in a shared perspective in a quite conscious way.

In a number of ways, through the use of rhythm and other syntactic devices as well as through written 'nudges', composers consciously used devices in the text which were intended to engage the reader. Awareness of the audience, made explicit for these composers because the scribe was modelling the role of audience to some extent, seemed to have enabled them to shape and control some of the uses of words and phrases in their stories with the express purpose of inviting the reader into a complicit and involved relationship with the composer.

This description of some of the features of the dictated story gives an indication of the ways in which these developing writers were beginning to deal with the constraints of written text.[13] Oral structures and language were still filtering through into their written text, particularly oral dialect forms of tenses and agreements of verb and antecedent. On several occasions though composers show that they have alternative, and more lexicalised, versions of dialect or colloquial words and phrases. Oral constructions also occur in the dialogue within the stories.

There is use of literary language and vocabulary in the stories both to create effect and to involve a reader or to 'nudge' them into a complicit relationship with the composer. These indications of written features which have been described give substance to the claim that the dictated story is an important bridge to written language which enables composers to tell stories using a discourse which has many of the features of written text.

Younger children also show awareness of this in their stories. James (8) dictated:

My brother William was the driver of the train.
He was a good driver but he was not a very good driver.

"Put very in big letters" he demanded.
Samantha's use of repetition:

she had to do all the cooking
she had to do all the washing

echoes similar devices in stories that were read to her.

A group poem dictated by some 8 year olds with reading difficulties contains words which certainly relate to their theme – The Haunted Churchyard – in a literary way.

In the middle of nowhere
A dark, dim churchyard lies . . . .
A coffin squeaks . . .
A rusty old bell in the clocktower
The creaking of cogs at midnight

It ends with the suitably chilling:

The phantom gardener arises
Carrying a deadly pair of shears . . .

You begin at this point to wonder how conscious that use of 'deadly' in the context of the graveyard is!

Good writers, writers who are motivated, are engaged with writing and absorbed into the process partly because of the enjoyment there is in playing with words to create effect and atmosphere. Novice writers and poor writers, incapacitated by their inability to handle handwriting and spelling at the same time as dealing with composition, can be set free to explore what writing is really like by using a scribe to help them encapsulate their ideas and their feelings. With older writers this can unlock for them the possibility of reflection and vicarious exploration of their inner feelings and emotions.

If consistent programmes, dealing with handwriting and spelling that are related to the needs and interests of what the writer wants and needs to say, are supporting the urge to write which has been triggered by seeing their own ideas and thoughts written down for them, then even those who have repeatedly experienced failure will gain the confidence and find the pleasure in using the resources for writing that they have within them. The output of literary stories, poems and articles from adult literacy groups bears witness to this possibility.

Chapter 5

Learning to organise and tell a story

Do dictated stories have the structure of 'real' stories so that they are valid as reading texts and as indications of the composer's potential for structuring written stories? What evidence is there that these are real stories and what kind of a framework is needed in order to determine this? Considering the differences between told and written stories makes it possible to identify some of the particular aspects of a dictated story[1] and to see whether there is a place for the dictated story between the oral and the written form. These stories were 'told', but told in a specific and intentional way because the composers knew that they were intended to be read, and because they watched the scribe write them down.

The stories were analysed in five areas to see whether the composers were aware of the need to organise and structure their stories like written stories. The main areas identified by Brewer were:

1 opening and closing procedures
2 the context of the story
3 the narrator's voice
4 the construction of characters
5 events and episodes.

Each of these areas will be looked at in detail using evidence from the research samples.

OPENING AND CLOSING PROCEDURES

In oral stories familiar openings signal to the audience that ordinary conversation has stopped and that the story has begun. In the same way endings wrap up the proceedings, often an epilogue with a moral or drawing conclusions is included in folk tales and fables. The predominant 'once upon a time' is used by many small children in order to start a story and 'they all lived happily ever after' to signal the end. Other endings often include 'I woke and it was all a dream' – maybe signalling re-entry into the world of reality as opposed to story.

In written stories there is freedom for the writer to choose how to open and close a story. In novels the first paragraph is often considered critical and the ending does not necessarily tie up all the loose ends.

In dictated stories the fact that the composers are telling their scribe they are beginning is often indicated by change of tone or intonation although the conventional opening may also signal the same fact. The reprise of the oral story, with its need to look back on events and reach some kind of conclusion, may also be present when a story is being dictated and there is a need to signal some kind of ending. Unlike more mature written stories there is no way in which dictated stories are easily composed out of sequence. The very fact of dictating probably precludes writing an ending first and then working backwards, although this is sometimes the practice in writing extended stories.

The most popular opening chosen by the sample group composers was 'One day' followed by a statement:

> *One day I went out on my bike*
> *One day a boy . . .*
> *One day there was a mum, a dad and two babies*
> *One day there was a man who loved beer*

Other openings also made time statements:

> *When I was ten we went on holiday in Devon*
> *It was ten o'clock at night*

Sometimes novice writers find it difficult to start. Graham and Andrew precipitate themselves into their stories:

> *Me and Robert went down the fairground*
> *A man pushed a woman into the road*

although later chapters open more smoothly:

> *The bell went in the morning and all the doors opened*
> *Robert went swimming this morning . . .*

The time marker is maybe a help in assuming the past tense and the formal voice of the teller. Younger children seem content to use: 'Once upon a time' but older writers may see this as babyish and substitute a time marker that is more specific.

Only one composer, Wayne, in *The CB Avengers* opened his story with a statement giving access to the composer's thoughts and feelings.

> *I had always wanted a CB because my mates had one.*

He also ended this story with a piece of dialogue:

> *If it hadn't been for you I wouldn't have had anything anyway.*

Wayne is using the autobiographical mode to tell a story in which he is both hero and the owner of the coveted CB equipment and so he handles his material by distancing it into the conventional story tense whilst retaining personalised opening and closing sentences. Other composers' endings were more parochial and prosaic, signalling the end but linking ending to familiar domestic or school routines.

> *We played all day and lived happily ever after*
> *They all had seen their Mum and Dad before they went over to the islands to settle and have families of their own*

The final chapter in several stories gave a sense of reprise, of tying up the ends. Most of the composers consciously devised openings and closings to their stories and several of them were content to use very convention-alised opening and closing procedures.

THE CONTEXT OF THE STORY

In the told story the story teller can make assumptions about a shared understanding of context, whether derived from earlier experiences of similar stories or because the social context is a shared one. In order to engage the imagination and feelings of the reader a written story context needs to be made at least minimally explicit, although, as Tannen[2] has pointed out, authors can depend on certain written down oral features in order to create an empathic response in the reader. In oral stories the teller often depends on a recognition of context in the listener. Conventionalised locations such as a cottage in the woods, the king's palace, the sacred mountain, are sufficiently familiar story scenarios for the listener to be able to construct a context for the story. In the dictated stories there was some shared social context in which the initial story was told. When composers did not identify a context it seems that they were relying on the listener and the eventual readers (who were of course themselves) to provide the context. Nearly all of these assumed contexts fell into the same category, being some kind of version of "going out", "coming in", "come round", "there" or some other implied place that was not so much the context of an event but rather an interim place to move to or from. Jason, in his description of the eagles flying to and from their nest, never actually mentions the word 'nest', making the assumption that his listener and reader will know what he means. Wayne is always "going out" or "coming in" – the assumed context of playing outside or re- turning inside being subsumed under the largely oral colloquialism "to go out", meaning to go out to play or to visit friends.

Sometimes very minimal contexts were given and these tended to be school, home or the names of particular shops or places. Those that were proper names, particularly those used by Mandy who located each of her ghosts at a local address, relied on the local knowledge of the reader in order for them to be understood. Less localised but important are contexts that 'set the scene'. Four days of the week or seasons are stated, e.g. "it was Sunday" but on ten occasions the time of the day in which the event is occurring is stated, e.g.

it was getting dark
It was 10 o'clock
nice and early
night (4 times)

The most common minimal context was "home" or "house", contexts which were used without amplification on 20 occasions. This reinforced the domestic quality of some stories with their

then I told my mum
I knocked for my friend

and similar parochial events and contexts.

Only Robert, describing his haunted house in the woods, comes close to using conventionalised contexts which are explicit to the reader because of their familiar story connotation. It may be that instructions to tell a story which had mentioned folk or fairy stories would have generated this kind of context.

It is sometimes difficult to make a clear distinction between a defined location and one which is still minimal although more than one word or short phrase. Contexts which mentioned the weather, nine in all, although often short set a context that is particularised and constructed by the composer. Such descriptions as:

the sun was out shining away
it was too wet to play out on my bike
outside it was pouring down with rain
it is wintertime and the snow is going to fall

seem to be a real attempt on the part of the composer to write so that the reader is able to construct the context in their own mind.

Some contexts not only relied on imagination but were also accurate and convincing. In contrast to Jason's eagles we find Lisa's otters in a carefully described environment:

a family of otters live in a sandbank by the sea . . . they live in a ditch which slopes into a hole . . . the hole is lined with leaves and grass so that it is safe and comfortable and warm for the babies

Throughout her story Lisa continued to construct a context for her story that was accurate but also conveyed a sense of fun and liveliness. The otters got lost in the river by taking the wrong turning as they got

washed away in the water . . . they went down a weir and splashed in the water below them'

Robert was also specific in his descriptions of place:

Colditz – it had big walls and gas chambers
through the cell window – it had iron bars – they could see the German guard on parade

In contrast other composers use little defined description and the reader is left with minimal clues as to the setting, e.g. "the cell", a "disco called Romance", "the pub" and "the fairground". When the composer has attempted to engage the reader in a shared emotion, to bring into play the involvement focus in the story, the story moves forward in a way which has elements of real literary quality:

They dodged out of the way and roosted in a forest. That's where they stayed it was dark that night . . . there was a moon shining in the window (Jason)
There was only two seats . . . Bozo sat on my lap and Nuisance sat on Crumple's lap. I rowed it into the water (Dawn)
At night I saw this big white bird coming towards the mountain (Paul)

Some contexts of the stories showed that the composers had difficulty in organising their material when accuracy of fact may not have been within their knowledge:

In 1947 the second world war began (Robert)
we landed in a desert . . . I rowed it into the water (Dawn)

Even so the reader is left with a sense of intention on the part of many of the composers to engage the readers' imagination and to share with them their own perceptions about where the events in their stories are taking place.

The composer of a dictated story is able to set a context, to describe and amplify a setting in such a way that the reader is able to imagine and share in the story context. On the other hand, perhaps because of the 'shared' nature of dictated stories, common contexts were often assumed. Composers of dictated stories do not rely only on oral strategies of conventionalised settings or shared contexts; in fact these older readers did not appear to want to use conventionalised settings at all, presumably because they were not felt to be appropriate to the sort of story they wanted to tell. Some composers of dictated stories were able to create contexts, through words and description, using accurate and emotive language in order to share thoughts and feelings with the reader.

THE ROLE OF THE NARRATOR IN DICTATED STORIES

In oral stories the narrator is obviously the person telling the story and, as such, has the opportunity of intruding on the listener with asides, suggestions, jokes, etc. Sometimes the narrator is the vehicle for telling the story in the persona of a character.[3] In written stories the narrator can also step out of character and speak to the reader, indicating an involvement focus in the story. It is possible that in dictated stories the encouragement to the scribe to get the composers to talk about themselves and their own experiences encouraged first person narration. In the narration it is also possible to see the extent to which the dictated story develops the common theme of wish fulfilment.[4] Many young story tellers choose to tell events or describe happenings which they feel may be proscribed or unacceptable in the detached third person, past tense.

Britton[5] suggests writing in the spectator role is an attempt to shape a picture of the world which then enables us to evaluate the experiences which we have had; narration styles may possibly indicate whether this is happening. The self which tells the story may reflect the degree of closeness and therefore real experience, or of distance and therefore fictionalised experience, of the composer.

Three composers chose to tell their stories consistently in the first person, although only Corinna maintained a factual account of events. She brought into the composing sessions articles such as airline tickets, menu and photographs which confirmed the 'real' nature of the experience she was narrating. Paul used his own experiences and knowledge to make a story about mountains and owls, transposing his knowledge into a more appropriate story setting than a London overspill New Town. Wayne, in a detailed account of daily life, maintained a 'real' narration until his second story. Here he began to imagine a way in which he might obtain the coveted CB – at the same time giving himself a competent and effective role in the story. It was unclear from Wayne's narrative whether he, as narrator, was in the role of Wayne, or whether "Wayne (my friend)" was a distancing of himself from the narrator role.

Three composers maintained a consistent third person story teller's voice throughout their stories. Darren and Andrew both wrote their first stories in the third person and then reverted to real experience in the second stories. Dawn and Graham experienced occasions on which the narrator's voice slid away from them and they mixed first and third person. Dawn changed the narrating voice halfway through, switching her third person narration of the story of Crumple and Nuisance and adding in Bozo, her own dog, and then swiftly taking over the narrator's voice herself. She had a bit of a muddle with:

> Bozo and Nuisance was walking behind them but Crumple and me did not know. I started to call . . .

but the rest of the story was told in the voice of "I", an "I" who was competent, coping and intelligent, who remembered the parachutes, planned and made the boat, rescued Crumple from the water and then returned in triumph to a dockside welcome in New York.

Jason also switched midway in *The Eagle Story* adding a note which sounded factual and convincing:

On the 28th May 1987 was when I last see the birds

In his second story, which was the narration of an action packed sequence of events, he used "we" to start nearly every sentence. In spite of this the content of the story bordered on the unacceptable with its

Real wicked

dummy and the frightening experience of "the little ones" when the dummy falls and

you could see its guts and brains fly all over the children

Perhaps for this reason he ended by telling the reader that

really it was water and invisible dye

He remained in control of the action but distanced himself from the reality of it by a cogent explanation.

The question of distancing was clearly seen in the story told by Andrew, *Scum*, which was based on a film which contained scenes of explicit and gratuitous violence. It was not just a straightforward rehash of the film but moved from one scene of violence to another. In personal exchanges with the scribe Andrew twice referred to violent scenes in his own life and it is possible to suggest that *Scum* was a story articulating some of his own frustrations and anxieties about violence.

It may be appropriate to note here that the story that some children dictate may well contain some kind of gratuitous violence. This may be due to unmediated and unsupervised video watching or reading of certain kinds of comics or it can, as in Andrew's case, seem to be a way of expressing deeply felt emotions. The dilemma remains of how to deal with this kind of writing. My experience has been that this first 'outburst' is often followed by lyrical or low key stories, as happened in Andrew's case when he composed a second five chapter story, called *The Fortune Teller*. Discussion will often also help composers to change aspects of their stories – particularly if an audience response is considered. My own feeling is that it is more important for such emotions to be expressed than suppressed, but that teachers and helpers are usually able to identify the child who is using violence as a way of gaining attention for reasons that are not genuine. Rehashing a film, using animals or fantasy characters or other ways of distancing are legitimate ways in which composers can get in touch with difficult or disturbing events. The use of mythic context as an enabling device is discussed in relation to girls in an article in *Beyond Words* (Smith 1994).

These composers were able to tell dictated stories with a consistent narrator's voice, whether they were first person stories based on real experience or fictionalised events and characters told in the third person. Many elements of the composers' own experiences were apparent in their stories, events, people and feelings from their own experience informing the events and characters in their stories. Some composers experienced difficulty in maintaining a consistent telling voice either from inexperience, or maybe from the difficulty of maintaining change of characters or events. The wish to enter the story as narrator seems to have been problematical on occasions, causing some mixing of the narrator's persona. Composers using the dictated story mode were capable of constructing consistent third person, past tense stories and also of maintaining a first person narrative, whether that narrative was consistent with their experience or was a fictionalised experience.

All of the stories, except those which retold the story of a film, contained elements which were identifiably of the composer's own experience and environment. As many of the first person narrators showed themselves in coping or superior situations it would seem that dictating a story is one way of extending upon and fictionalising one's own experience. Some stories did appear to deal with emotions and experiences that were disturbing or difficult and there was an element of distancing in these stories which might have related to a wish to explore such areas in the safety of fiction.

CHARACTERS AND CHARACTERISATION IN THE DICTATED STORY

The creation and use of characters in narrative is considered to be an integral part of the construction of a story.[6] From an early age children develop expectations about characters in stories, although the ability to distinguish real from fictional does not develop in some children until 7 or 8 years old. These expectations and conventions mean that readers and tellers can infer certain characteristics in a story's characters just by the choice of character type, e.g. the witch, the stepmother, the youngest of three sons. This conventional characterisation in some early story telling and writing may be sufficient indication to the reader of the kind of actions to expect and the way in which they may be likely to identify with characters in the story.

The creation of characters to demonstrate the 'heroic' nature of the composer or to address, in fictional form, situations which in real life are threatening and disturbing[7] may determine for some composers the kind of characters they will use in their story. Equally they may feel safe with the 'stock' character from which they assume the reader will derive the message they wish to send. It is interesting to consider what function a character has in a plot. Do the characters exist in order to perform the actions or do the actions characterise the person? It is possible for the reader to come to 'know' the character without a straightforward description being given.

The composers in these two samples were inexperienced writers and readers. Apart from stories read to them and the lower stages of reading schemes they had not had access to many stories to read for themselves. The expectation might be that they would use many of the undefined stock characters that Applebee found in his study of the told stories of young children. The other source of knowledge of character available to these composers was gained from their experience of television and film characters. They were all avid 'soap' followers and discussed the characters in great detail – having characters that were their favourites and those they disliked. Characters from television and film might be expected to occur in some of their stories. The instruction to the scribes to encourage composers to talk about their own experiences might encourage them to use themselves as characters in their stories.

In the told story the realisation of character is often achieved through performance. The gestures, facial expressions, intonation and body language of the story teller cues the listeners in to the characters in the story. The listener's response to character is partly manipulated by the face-to-face interaction with the story teller. In a written story hints, responses and understanding of characters in the story need to be made explicit for the reader so that they can share the author's own perception of how the character 'ticks'.

Some composers made little attempt to differentiate between characters occurring in their stories other than to say:

> *the bloke*
> *the pals*
> *the man*
> *my mates*
> *my friends*
> *the police*

For many composers such minimal signals to differentiate character seemed to be sufficient. Robert had great difficulty in settling on a focus for his *Colditz Story*. Having in mind, no doubt, the multiplicity of characters in the film, none of them with particularly memorable names, he referred to the main character in the plural of "the pals". The protagonists were guards, patrols and officers variously, and the prefix German was enough to differentiate them as "the enemy". Other composers used descriptions that tended to be minimal, but at least showed the beginning of the need to flesh out character for the reader:

Tracey, my brother's girlfriend . . . she takes hours to do her hair
Stephen, my brother . . . he's greedy

Proper names were used usually only to demarcate. Mum and Dad, occurring frequently, were in fact stock characters as so little differentiation between one Mum and Dad and another occurred. The conscious naming of characters was perhaps one step on the way to description of characters as individuals. Mandy called all her characters after the real names of friends and members of her family – this is a shared joke in some instances, such as the marrying off of the Special Needs Coordinator in the school to the headmaster! The chapter named a different ghost each time and also gave at least an indication of the characteristics about to be described. Wayne, in *CB Avengers*, took great delight in the 'handles' he created for his characters

Superman
Ace-Race
Casual Kid

Dawn created the homely, kindly character of Crumple and the naughty dog Nuisance, their names reflecting the kind of character they were. She used the folk-tale "Stiltskin" first to describe Crumple's next door neighbour and then presumably took on that persona herself as narrator, although she did not make this very clear in the story. The dog Bozo, companion to the naughty Nuisance, completed a group whose names alone give a flavour of the story to come. In the same way Peepee, Sweep and Neepee, the energetic, naughty and adventurous otters, their names anticipating the squeaky, mischievous nature of the trio, seemed to be aptly named with the composer intending to create a sense of character by the choice she had made.

Most of the composers do not seem to see the necessity for using names as anything other than demarcators of one character from another. This in itself causes confusion which they often resolve by using "this man" or "my friend's dad" or "another man" or similar common nouns as differentiating descriptions, a device common in children's early writing attempts. Some composers do seem to understand that naming is a form of description and their characters and their names have a similarity which is likely to trigger off expectations about the character in the reader's mind. The lack of definition in naming characters in the stories may be an indication that many of the persona appearing in the story are not integral to either action or meaning. Several of the composers introduce characters with undifferentiated names who appear momentarily and then are never referred to again.

There may be a relationship between the number of characters and the complexity of the story.[8] To some extent this may well be true, sequencing of many events and characters in the story taking considerable organisation and attention. The minimal description of a character, name and indication of function, may be all that is necessary if that character is only, in T. S. Eliot's words:

> . . . one that will do
> To swell a progress, start a scene or two
>
> (*The Love Song of J. Alfred Prufrock*)

To this extent then the number of characters and the extent to which they are described is of importance in written stories which rely on written description for arousing the feelings and attention of the reader.

Immature composers may need to people their stories with rather nebulous characters in order to keep the thread of where the story is going. In oral stories repetition, parallel events and paralinguistically differentiated characters help the audience to perceive characteristics and to keep cognisance of what is going on. The attempt to write down some features of their story presented these composers with a difficulty. Because their stories were written down they were able to tell complicated stories, but they obviously found it difficult to describe or enumerate too many characters. It then became easier to refer to simplistic characters such as "everybody ran out screaming", "this other man" in order to keep the flow of the story going. Attempts at signalling that this "man" was different from another already mentioned such as:

> *another man* (Andrew)
> this other boy (Graham)
> a kid next to me (Darren)
> one of the pals (Robert)

would seem to indicate the beginning of an understanding that a reader needs help in sorting out who everybody is. Scribe support in clarifying these kinds of confusions by asking questions which indicated that they were confused was one of the ways in which the composers came to realise the need to differentiate between a large cast of characters.

Few characters drawn straight from traditional characterisation were found in the stories, although Robert has a "devil" and "Frankenstein" in his *Haunted House* and a "ghost" in the *Haunted Oil Rig*. The influence of film was evident in both Andrew and Robert's stories with their clear differentiation between good and evil forces; and although the reader may feel that both sides in Andrew's "Scum" were in fact as bad as each other, it was obvious that the composer's sympathy lay with Spider and that Andrew viewed him as the hero of the story. The familiar archetype of the 'bad' German is employed by Robert, and "the pals", both collectively and occasionally singly, are set in the heroic role in opposition to the Germans. In *The Haunted Oil Rig* a "man" appears who "tests" the ghosts, and this seems to have some connection with *Ghostbusters*, a film current at the time of Robert writing this story.

There are a number of ways in which differentiation and development of a character can take place in a story. Writers can describe how characters look, their behaviour, their conversation and give access to their thinking. The way in which action in a story occurs is either integrally as a result of the kind of character who then precipitates the actions, or peripherally, as when characters 'perform' actions which seem to be external to them and over which they have little control. Some of these characteristics are picked up by the reader from minimal cues in the text. Very little description of how characters looked was given in the stories. Dawn gave a clear description of Crumple:

he was a very tall skinny man

and Andrew described one of Spider's victims as

the black man . . . . a big strong coloured man

Clear descriptions of the owls were given by Paul, although he gave no indication of how any of his people looked. We know that his owl

had lines on the wings and the tail was brown but normally it would be white

and that the dog Bozo in Dawn's *Nuisance the Dog*

was a brownish-blackish colour

Robert had little differentiating description in his *Colditz Story* apart from the early description of the pilot of the Lancaster, the co-pilot, and the three machine gunners:

the pilot was slightly injured to the head and leg. And the co-pilot had a broken arm and he had a splint round it with two pieces of wood . . . one had a metal bar on top of him and one was slightly injured to the hand and the other one was shot in the head

Other composers did differentiate some of their characters, but the indication given to the reader was through the behaviour of the character. All of Mandy's different ghosts were differentiated by their behaviour. Some of their behaviour was obsessional – for sweets, for beer, for ice-cream – and this obsession brought about their death and subsequent transformation into ghosts. Other ghosts had an accident through an activity they were doing – Graham in the swimming pool, Dennis falling off a ladder whilst painting and Peter and Linda, the Holiday Ghosts, falling overboard as they quarrelled about which boat they should be on. On other occasions she gave some insight into character through dialogue.

The old lady who kept the pub next to the Painting Ghost had a nice line in chat:

> *Come in I'm not stopping you . . . I might pop up and see Mr. Jackson and see if he can run me up the town.*
> *Quick come round there's an emergency in my house*

which contributes to her character. On another occasion there were glimpses into the feelings of a character. Graham, the Sporting Ghost,

> *. . . couldn't understand why people kept running away from him it made him sad.*

Jason tells us that "Squawker" who fell out of the nest couldn't fly because he hadn't been training:

> *(he) couldn't be bothered with training so he left it*

There was not much evidence of intention to share perceptions or feelings with the reader, although in those stories where the narrator's voice was autobiographical there was a sense of a person coming through. Corinna conveyed her excitement, her interest in everything, her disgust with foreign food, her longing to get home and give her presents to her friend Nicky. Paul gave an impression of an earnest and informed bird watcher, anxious to do the right thing – only in his description of the baby owl "nicking" his mother's dinner did he add a little lightness and humour to the story.

In spite of the complicated story line and the kaleidoscope of events in Graham's story the characters of Graham, Robert and Robert's mum were conveyed to the reader. Robert, loud mouthed and cocksure

> *'What are you waiting for Christmas?'*
> *so Robert said 'Grooooowl' a growling noise*

made Graham's mother cry but was no match for his own mother who "kills him" and sends everyone to bed. It was in the final chapter of Graham's story, with its confrontation between Graham and the boys who "take the mick" and the mixture of jail, family fights and eventual death that the mixture of violence and compassion in Graham's 'narrator' was shown most clearly.

Dawn had a cast of clearly drawn characters, speaking with different voices. The slightly querulous Crumple:

> *Crumple was beginning to like the poor little puppy until he heard him underneath the bed*
> *This is the worst day of my life*

contrasted with the chirpy Stiltskin:

I quite enjoyed it. Anyway my teeth look quite nice after eating those seven apples

Dawn's characters and the otters of Lisa's story were the means by which the action in the story took place. Lisa's otters' teasing ended in a fight where

They all had some red scratches on their bodies

The reader has a sense of knowing these characters, of seeing the action through their eyes, of being involved with them. When Jason tells the readers his dad was a boy scout so

he had a magnifying glass with him

and that

the sun was shining away and my Dad was sunbathing as usual

there is a sense of his Dad's character, and the subsequent lighting of the fire and the lunch at 8 o'clock in the evening come as no surprise.

EVENTS AND EPISODES

The primary task of the story teller is the articulation and organisation of the events and episodes in time which move towards a resolution. The telling of these events and episodes is the recreation of 'virtual experience', the construing of the story teller's own experience and the movement from the world of the realistic and known towards distant and then fantastical lands. The way in which the story teller organises these events and resolutions moves hand in hand with the way in which language is used to articulate the plot.[9]

In written stories the discourse structure does not have to follow the sequence of events in real or imagined time. Flashforward and flashback are often used to create effect, real time can be contrasted with 'in the head' thinking or philosophising. Dictated stories, however, being composed in an oral mode, might be expected to follow the pattern of events and episodes in oral stories where the order of the discourse follows the order of the events in real or imagined time.

The majority of the events described in the dictated stories followed the order of the events within the time sequence of the story. The exceptions seemed to be more in the order of parenthetical statements:

this did not mean just to go up and down and get their two children's food . . . .
his brother couldn't be bothered
On the 28th May 1987 was when I last see the birds . . . . I was there with my Mum

being additions to the described event structure in Jason's stories, giving reasons and adding information. Such loops in the narrative, inviting the reader to have more information or come closer to the teller in some way, are similar to the 'nudges' found in involvement-focused discourse. They are interruptions to the main discourse which explain or underline the significance of events that are taking place. At one point Robert described two parallel events happening at the same time. He introduced them both with the word "meanwhile"

> *meanwhile at the prison the German guards were questioning everybody . . .*
> *meanwhile at the German post on the shore . . .*

This was the nearest that any composer got to the idea of flashforward or flashback. Most of the discourse followed the underlying event structure although there were instances in which the story was interrupted in order to clarify a point or to underline why an event has occurred in the story.

In many oral stories, particularly those of folk origin, there is a sequence of events that is repeated, sometimes successfully, sometimes unsuccessfully, or else developed in a similar way. Examples of this might be the succession of people trying to fit on Cinderella's shoe, or different groups of people attempting to solve a problem or find a treasure. These repetitive structures help the teller to sequence events and give the listener expectations of the next event in a sequence and how it is likely to be introduced by the teller. Since dictated stories were composed and told orally some of these structuring devices might have been expected to have been present in the stories. On the other hand, the fact that the stories were written down and therefore were available for reflection and recall might mean that these structures were not felt necessary or appropriate for the composers.

Most of the composers structured their events by reference to time: "next day", "near to Christmas", "next morning", "a week later". This device seems to be sufficient for most to allow them to carry on their narrative in a sequential way. Some repetitive structuring of events and parallel development take place in the dictated stories. The repetitive themes in Mandy, Graham, Paul and Andrew's stories seem to be similar to elements in their own real lives. There may be elements in some dictated stories that are repeated because they are a way in which the composers are construing events which occur or worry them in their real lives. There is little evidence that such structures as the rule of three occur as structuring devices in the dictated stories of these older composers. Only Lisa has a family of three similar to the three sons found in Western fairy tales. Most composers seemed able to structure their stories by relying on time sequences although some introduced repetition of structures or of motifs. Some powerful motifs such as fights or money were the recurring events around which the stories were structured.

The analysis of these dictated stories and their structures showed that dictated stories were often still close to many of the features of oral stories. This is perhaps to be expected. Betty Rosen[10] found that practice in story telling was a potent starting point for writing a story for pupils who were poor at writing.

CLASSROOM IMPLICATIONS

Younger children seem to be closer to familiar story line, often content to retell familiar stories. Their drawings may be more uninhibited and detailed, giving them a richer resource for telling about their characters. Individual or group stories are often precipitated by drawing, and questioning by the scribe helps to elicit details. Young children particularly seem to enjoy putting their friends or family into their stories. Samantha (6) told both her stories about her friends. Kirsty lived all on her own:

she had to do all the washing, she had to do all the cooking.

In her next story she puts in her boyfriend and her best friend Marcia. She and the boyfriend are king and queen and Marcia is invited to the birthday party

with cakes, and buns

The drawing and detailed description of their clothes (Figure 9) is very similar to Samantha's favourite game in the home corner where she dresses up in a long lurex dress, high heels and handbag and dispenses tea to imaginary friends at a tea party. Samantha is the eldest of four children. Perhaps her fictionalised world of elegance and romance is an important 'alternative world' in which to create her stories.

When Gary embarked on his story of *The Three Silly Bears* he used some of the structures from the original familiar story but transposed them into the world of the bears that he had created:

It was time for Baby Bear to go to school. He didn't want to go.
He ran into the school.
He went to his class but he didn't like it. It was too big.
So they put him in a middle-sized class.
But he didn't like it.
Then he went to cookery class and he showed them all how to make porrige.
The teacher thought it was a good improvement.

Kirsty (7), retelling the story of the pirates and the angel from a picture book with no words, creates characters based only on her own interpretation of the pictures.

They had cakes and there was
some buns.
Kirsty came and she looked
pretty and Marsha came. She
weared white high heels.
They played pass-the -parcel and
musical statues and musical
bumps.

Figure 9 Part of Samantha's story, and her drawing

The angel woke and runned and saw the ship.
The pirate was asleep and one pirate was snoring.
She found the soldier tied up on a rope.
Then she saw him and she untied the rope with a knife.
After when she opened it the soldier kissed her. Then they creeped downstairs
so the pirates wouldn't hear.
. . . Then the police came and got them (the pirates) and they were sent to jail
because they had been so naughty stealing money from the pig!

When groups of children compose together the thread or sequence of the story is often determined by drawing – maybe they will draw first, maybe, as in the case of the group stories about Friday 13th and the disaster at sea, the central coordinating factor is a large sheet of paper on which a map is drawn (see Chapter 1).

Younger children often attempt to write about the film story running through their heads. It is the basis of much inarticulate and incoherent writing when they try to convey the story of the film without making contexts or characters explicit because they can 'see it in their mind'. Marcus's first dictated story was about goodies and baddies and even he was confused on trying to reread it. Using photographs to sequence a story, and focusing it on him, made all the difference to his motivation and his ability to read back his story.

Danny's (10) first attempt was even worse. It was called *Batman and the Robbers* and included an odd robber who kept money upstairs in a bank in a wardrobe. It was halfway through a very unsuccessful second dictating session that it was realised that he was writing about Batman and Robin and that the scene was an unmediated bit of a film. No wonder Danny couldn't read back what he had written! In fact in his Special School it was felt that Danny was never going to read or be able to make sense of things. He couldn't even look at a lit gas ring on the top of the stove and colour in the correct circle on his work sheet. However, there was something that Danny did know about. It was his present of a picture of his bike that made me realise that we were trying to make stories about the wrong kind of subject. When I wrote down what he did know about, himself and his beloved bike, the text was well structured, sequential and made sense (Figure 10). More importantly, Danny could read it and it was this story which made the breakthrough in his reading and understanding.

Many younger children and children with learning difficulties may need to start with their own experience. The narrator's voice then becomes clearly the voice of the author in charge of the story and characterisation and events are subsumed under their telling of a real experience. Many older children want to tell their own experiences in a fictionalised version, and this seems to be a positive and important aspect of making sense of their own life stories.

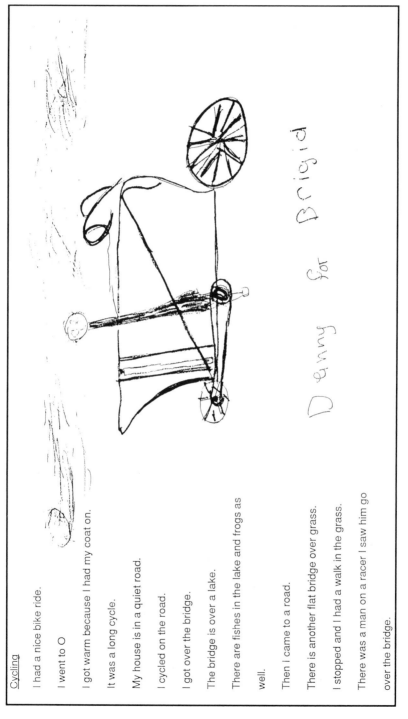

Cycling

I had a nice bike ride.

I went to O

I got warm because I had my coat on.

It was a long cycle.

My house is in a quiet road.

I cycled on the road.

I got over the bridge.

The bridge is over a lake.

There are fishes in the lake and frogs as well.

Then I came to a road.

There is another flat bridge over grass.

I stopped and I had a walk in the grass.

There was a man on a racer I saw him go over the bridge.

Figure 10 The breakthrough for Danny – a picture and story about his bike

Clive (14), when he wrote about the children's home and his school experiences, came to terms with some of the things in his life he wasn't able to talk about in a story which had 22 chapters, well-constructed characters, many well-described contexts and a use of language that was powerful and effective. After a conflict with the woodwork teacher, for example, he is able to 'write out' his feelings of anger and frustration in an exceedingly funny way. Clive and friends are being told off in the headmaster's office when:

> *Mrs. Orwin came in. She was a tall, lanky woman with messy hair. She came in all worried saying someone had broken their leg. It was a teacher.*
> *"What do you mean? What has happened? Who was it?" yelled Mr. Street.*
> *"Someone working on the roof on top of the woodwork block dropped a large pole and knocked him over. Another fell on him and broke his leg"*
> *"Why haven't you phoned for an ambulance?" said Mr. Street.*
> *"I've phoned already" said Mrs. Orwin, "not for nothing have I got my St. John's Ambulance Certificate . . ."*
> *In the playground everyone was talking and laughing about it. In the hospital Mr. Green (the woodwork master) was lying in agony. He had five injections.*

Here we see not only a writer using fiction to mediate his experiences but a boy, previously inarticulate and unable to write, using words in a powerful and effective way.

Many authors seem to need to 'write out' feelings of violence and aggression, maybe the result of unmediated video 'nasties' or else coming to terms with their own feelings of aggression, anger or unhappiness. These violent stories often seem to be followed by a second story in which there is a much more rational and personalised context as in the case of Andrew and his stories *Scum* and *The Fortune Teller* (see p. 66).

Some authors need an alter ego in which to explore the feelings of competence, leadership or success. Sometimes this is a character taken from a film – Mark (12) wrote a series of books about himself as "The Hulk" – or it relates to a particular interest – Matthew (11) wrote many stories about fishing and his competition wins, Lisa (13) stories about horses, Dean (11) about his trip to Australia complete with maps, timetables for aeroplanes, shipping routes, surfing, etc. Harry (8) was prepared to co-operate only if his book was about insects, and Claire (8) told her story about how to shoot pheasants with many examples and illustrations!

Other writers may explore disturbing or unhappy aspects of their lives through a literary context. Lorrainne (14) dictated a long story about a time-slip in which a poor, ragged child (with shades of *Water Babies*) became excluded from a 'posh' school, mirroring her own feeling of exclusion and isolation in school and maybe dealing with some of her feelings of hurt. It would be unusual to find a child or group of children who do not have a story to tell.

Most teachers are aware of the difficulties inexperienced writers have in constructing their stories in a sequential or coherent way. Lack of practice in sustaining a length of text, difficulties with handwriting and spelling all interfere with the process of telling a story. Using their dictated stories to extend their understanding of structures, the way in which texts 'hang together' and how to compose an interesting story can give inexperienced writers the opportunity to develop their ability to organise and structure a story even before they are able to write it for themselves. This can be particularly helpful for bright poor readers or frustrated or limited writers.

WAYS IN WHICH TEACHERS MIGHT EXTEND AND SUPPORT THE DEVELOPMENT OF STORY STRUCTURE

There have been suggestions that 'too much' dictated story might result in boring and bland reading texts. Although considerable evidence now suggests that this is unlikely to be so, there is no doubt that teachers can develop strategies for extending children's understanding of story structure and characterisation which will help them to become aware of the ways in which stories are structured and to extend their own ability to tell the story.

Ways of helping composers to develop the characters in a story

The characters in the story can be described during the process of writing as part of the planning process; alternatively, experience of thinking about how characterisation works can come as a result of reflection on the characters in an existing story, whether dictated or conventional. Lists of characters can be made and then considered as if they were a cast of a play, with specific characteristics described. A Venn diagram can be made showing overlapping characteristics, or characters can be considered against a matrix of characteristics (Figure 11).

	Kind	Angry	Likes Children
Mrs. Brown			
Jill			
Policeman			
Wendy			

Figure 11 A table to help plan characters and their characteristics

Making a web in which episodes are put on the inside and characters on the outside may help some writers to think about the relationship of character to action (Figure 12).

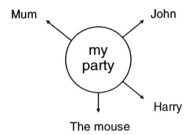

Figure 12 A web relating characters to action

Ways of telling the story

There are many different ways of telling a story but children are not always aware of this. This may account for the repetitive opening and closing procedures and narrator's voice in many stories. Examples and practice in 'telling it a different way' can increase the author's repertoire. Widening this experience involves an understanding that stories have a teller – something that less-experienced readers may not fully under-stand. Reflecting on the role of the teller, both in their own stories and in stories that are read to them, will help children to gain this experience. Figure 13 suggests possible starting points for such reflection.

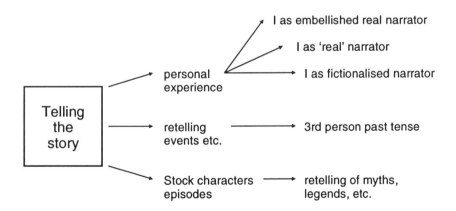

Figure 13 Some ways of telling a story

Events and episodes: some ways of supporting development

Support can be given to inexperienced writers by structuring the sequences for them. Possible ways of doing this include:

1 Drawing pictures first.
2 Planning using a flow chart.
3 Planning using pictures.
4 Planning using a web with the setting in the middle and characters and happenings on the outside.
5 Making chapters from a list of main events.
6 Making a time line of the plot: what went before, what happened, what came next?
7 Storyboarding as if for a television or pictorial production.
8 Scripting as if for a play.
9 Producing a comic strip.

Extending an understanding of story structure

Focusing attention on the way in which stories are structured can help the inexperienced writer to understand the ways in which stories are structured and the ways in which writers get particular effects.

Ways of focusing attention could include:

1 Looking at different beginnings and endings in stories and talking about them.
2 Deconstructing a story into characters, episodes and events.
3 Identifying the main points in a story – what changes things? – what makes things happen?
4 Looking closely at characters in a story and then making posters, identikits, passports.
5 Writing/dictating letters from characters describing events.
6 Interviewing characters and role-playing important events in the story.

All these activities for extending understanding of story structure could be group or class activities in which children with limited writing capability use a scribe or work in a supportive group. The texts for use can be dictated texts used in the classroom as well as conventional books.

Group stories for inexperienced writers and readers

Group stories often work best when they involve journeys, adventures or situations in which the group members themselves can figure (Figure 14).

However they approach composing their story some children will need help with relating the use of words and structuring a story to their own experience. They need to start with a simple story that they know

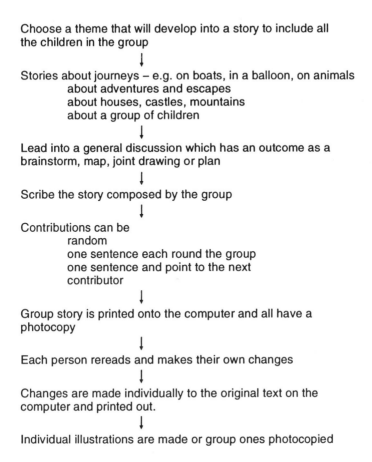

Choose a theme that will develop into a story to include all
the children in the group
↓
Stories about journeys – e.g. on boats, in a balloon, on animals
          about adventures and escapes
          about houses, castles, mountains
          about a group of children
↓
Lead into a general discussion which has an outcome as a
brainstorm, map, joint drawing or plan
↓
Scribe the story composed by the group
↓
Contributions can be
          random
          one sentence each round the group
          one sentence and point to the next
          contributor
↓
Group story is printed onto the computer and all have a
photocopy
↓
Each person rereads and makes their own changes
↓
Changes are made individually to the original text on the
computer and printed out.
↓
Individual illustrations are made or group ones photocopied

Figure 14 Producing a group story

and gradually work towards more fictionalised accounts. Other writers
revel in the opportunity to create alternative worlds in which they or their
characters can feature. In these worlds heroes and heroines can overcome
all obstacles, villains can be of the wickedest hue, solutions can be
magical or unexpected. Some children will prefer to work on sequencing
and constructing a book which is non-fiction rather than story based.

Facilitating extended writing by using a scribe and creating dictated
texts allows inexperienced writers to get to grips with the processes
involved in constructing a text and in sequencing writing, controlling
plot and inventing or ordering characters and episodes. In this way they
get to understand the purposes of writing and, as a reader of their own
writing, they learn to reflect on the effectiveness of what they have

composed, to edit and change it where necessary and to focus on other writers' work in order to see how story organisation works.

In all cases the fact of being in control of character, event and telling gives confidence and allows novice writers to glimpse the immense possibilities that await the author in the world of words and story.

Possible outcomes

One Big Book for shared reading and individual books
Story illustrated by individuals to make a complete book
Frieze for the wall or reading corner
Zig-zag books or other books with flaps, pulls
Making a board game to accompany the story
Turning the story into different genres:

Newspaper
Play
Interview
Broadcast
Poem
Information book

Chapter 6

Classroom approaches

When the components of the triangle are present – competent writer as scribe/listener, a composer who wants to write a text and a text to be written – then there are endless possibilities for using this approach. The following case studies were undertaken in the course of normal school activities, sometimes individually and sometimes with a small group or even a whole class of children. Where possible other relevant literacy activities are indicated. Composing and reading your own story is not an end in itself. The ultimate goal is to make independent, confident and competent writers and readers. For some children this is a long-term goal which will take many years of patient, incremental work to achieve. For others, seeing what they are able to achieve, practising reading on real texts and having a sense of control through knowing and understanding the strategies they are using can be the necessary breakthrough into literacy. Children unable to read and write, particularly as they get older, are doubly handicapped. They cannot express ideas, feelings and knowledge and make them their own through writing and neither have they easy access to the vicarious life of feeling and knowledge through books. By making books with them we allow both of these important aspects of literacy to be effectively addressed.

The evidence has been given for progress and confidence in reading and for a real engagement with the skills of composing through dictating and reading dictated texts. These more informal and sometimes short-term classroom projects are just an indication of the possibilities inherent in this approach to literacy in the classroom.

THE NECESSARY COMPONENTS

The small selection of examples shown in Figure 15 is chosen to try and cover as wide a range of composers as possible. The actual example is described and the classroom implications and possibilties are discussed.

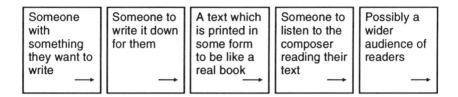

Figure 15 The necessary components for classroom projects

SMALL GROUP OF INFANTS MAKING A COLLABORATIVE TEXT

Some stories were made by five children who were making little or no progress in reading and writing. The reasons for their difficulties were varied: three were children who were slow to progress and had limited literacy experience and the other two, Simon and Josh, had particular difficulties which are discussed in the next section. All the children wrote individual stories as well as taking part in two group activities with dictated texts central to them but with other literacy activities arising from the activities.

Red Riding Hood group activity

The class topic was fairy stories, so materials that related to the topic were produced by the group for other members of the class (see Figure 16).

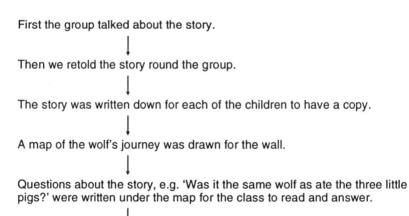

Figure 16 Red Riding Hood group activity

Little Red Riding Hood

Red Riding Hood	wolf	big	bad
Grandmother	a	the	house
through	for	he	she
basket	lived	forest	path
hiding	walk	along	went
with	saw	flowers	was
picking	frightened	in	long
Next line	Rub out	space	capitals

Figure 16 Continued

As a group they talked, retold the story which was written down for them to read and illustrate, then used the words and the story in order to make the map. The map was a tangible prop from which to raise the questions. They wrote the questions down for others to read. Using the concept keyboard with whole words, some with picture cues, on the overlay enabled them to write their own story and to have it printed. In this way the use of the computer was encouraged and they completed a story.

INDIVIDUAL TEXTS

A look at the two very differing texts written by Simon and Josh will indicate the kind of story work done with the children individually. This individual work can more closely relate to particular needs.

Simon: a child with perceptual and motor difficulties

Simon (6) had severe difficulties. He couldn't recognise letters, copy letters or recognise text unless it was very familiar, although he had a good oral vocabulary and was able to talk with some degree of fluency. He had a lot of story knowledge as his parents read to him frequently and he was able to dictate a story about the characters from *Ghostbusters* to his scribe without any difficulty. His story is literary and well constructed and contains some elements of humour (Figure 17). Typed out with a specialist font he was delighted by how it looked "Like a real book". The story was taped for him so that he could listen many times and he was encouraged to read with the tape and to point to the words. Work with a boy like Simon is very long term but motivation and finding texts that engage his long-term interest and can act as a springboard for other literacy work is of great importance. His dictated story seemed to be going to do this.

Dictation → Printed text → Shared reading → Reading with tape

Fear of failure and reading refusal

Josh (6) was in the same class as Simon. Quiet and shy with adults, where reading was concerned he was entirely passive and just refused to engage with any text. The eldest of four boys, he was the playground menace, finding it hard to relate to other children and resorting to much fighting and bullying. He was encouraged to draw after a lot of talk about his family and his new baby brother (Figure 18). He was delighted to find his drawings and his "explanation", which was not a story but sentences

One day Peter Bankman was having a
shower.

When he came out he grabbed
SLIMER, the goody ghost, instead of a
towel.

He picked **SLIMER** up and slimed his
face.

He wanted to get dry but he slimed
instead!

SLIMER YELLED!

Figure 17 Part of Simon's *Ghostbusters* tale

giving the name and age of each person in his family, returned to him as
a book. It was a minimal text but one in which he was engaged and
interested and that he didn't view as a reading book in the school sense.
For a child like Josh getting started is the first step towards reading. He
could not take the risk of failing with 'school' reading, but viewing his
own story as different he was able to use the things he had picked up
about reading in a positive and safe way.

Talk   →   Drawing   →   Statements about   →   Reading
                        the pictures   the text

Many children seem to suffer from this particular fear of failing. Often
they may be particularly sensitive to the peer group assessment of them.
Disturbed or aggressive behaviour is a way in which they try to redress
the balance, to maybe make themselves acceptable to the group. Listening
to older children talking about how they feel when they fail at reading:

"I'm all burned up inside"
"I want to go away and hide"
"They think you're an idiot sort of thing and its only that you can't
read"

makes it quite clear that the public and obvious nature of reading failure
is one of the reasons why children retreat from the activity either by
extreme passivity – refusal or over-dependence on others to help – or by
diversions caused by bad behaviour or clowning. Drawing attention
away from the reading is done by any means.

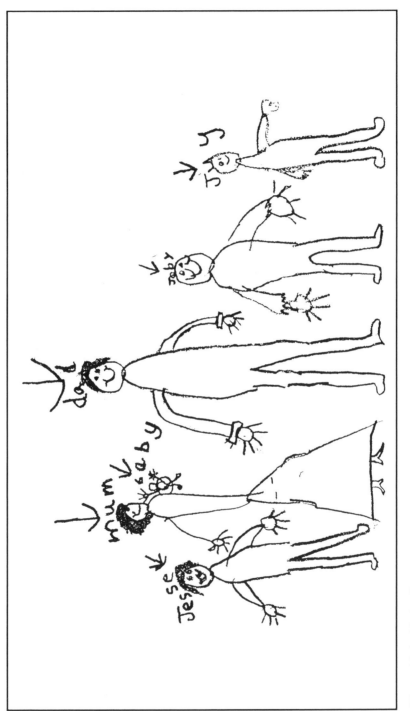

Figure 18 Josh's family

THE WAY IN WHICH SHORT-TERM WORK WITH A STORY CAN GIVE SOME CHILDREN A NEW START

Johnny (10) was one of the few children in a small school who was not reading 'up to standard'. He was given remedial help which consisted of reading infant school texts with a support teacher in the entrance hall to the school. A large child for his age, this public exposure of his weakness was causing him extreme pain and he reacted with surly and un-cooperative behaviour. The response from his school was to try and persuade his parents that he needed to go to a special school.

At the first session with Johnny there was no eye contact, neither would he answer any questions. He did, however, nod an agreement to come back another day to make a book about skateboarding, which his mother said was a favourite activity.

On the next occasion he came on his skateboard and Polaroid photographs were taken of him as he arrived. These were used as a basis for the story, which was typed straight onto the computer so that he could go home with a print-out. His book was made over four short sessions and then it was arranged that he would swop a copy of his book with another boy (Matthew) that a student was working with.

His story showed how engaged and positive he could be when the subject interested him, and how well he was able to use written forms of language. An extract from his letter to Matthew shows an interesting insight into his gain in confidence and sense of himself as an author.

Are you going to write a book to me or are you not? I would like to see your book and how much you have written. You might not be able to read my book I have written so much.

Short-term work like this cannot claim miraculous 'cures' but what it does do is give the child a new start, reclaim for them some dignity and sense of achievement and show them that they are able to read.

Many children know much more about reading than they demonstrate. Given a text that is predictable and which they can read and self-correct with confidence because it is their own language and idiom, they put into operation the dormant understandings about reading that they have acquired, often through years of remedial input. For many older readers this experience of being able to read, particularly when the text is substantial and includes plenty of reading practice as a result, does generalise to a more confident, positive and active approach to reading.

SUPPORTING LANGUAGE WORK WITH A DOWN'S SYNDROME CHILD

Sam (10) is a relaxed, interested and conscientious learner. He has poor sight, limited hearing and others have difficulty understanding what he is trying to say although he communicates freely and his speech is supported by intonation and a great ability to act out and mimic happenings. Sam's story was built up around photographs taken of himself and his family (Figure 19). The text is very limited and Sam may not necessarily learn to read it for himself. Nevertheless it is 'himself in a book', making the process of reading more obvious and individualised. Pleasure in turning pages, pointing and recognising may over time build into the ability to recognise and read words and sentences. At school his teacher made a similar book using photographs taken on Sam's holiday.

Again, using photographs, it is possible to support a story such as Sam's book by making concept keyboard overlays on which the photographs are put. When the photograph is touched, printed messages appeared on the screen.

The concept keyboard can be programmed so that there are incremental texts for the screen. As a first example the photographs would generate only naming words. Touching each photograph in the first programme SAM 1 would generate the words

Sam
Ruth
Big Sam

A second programme, SAM 2, would generate a sentence when each photograph was touched.

I am Sam
Ruth is my sister
Sam is a strong boy

Further texts might include words and sentences from Sam's story. Using such personalised texts can make the task of reading more accessible to some children as well as giving practice with overlearning vocabulary which is contextualised in meaning and interest.

GAINING THE CONFIDENCE TO PUT READING STRATEGIES INTO PRACTICE

Dean (11) came to secondary school from a primary school for children with learning difficulties. He had a reputation for unpredictable and violent rages which were particularly precipitated by anything to do with reading and writing. He came to a comprehensive school, initially for a trial period, because of his distress at being at a special school and his mother's determination to help him to succeed. His elder brother was already at a senior special school. Dean was a tense, nervous boy whose

Figure 19 Photographs of Sam and his sister – the basis for a story

intelligence was obvious straight away. He learned the layout of the school, names of teachers and protocols immediately.

His special timetable had to include building up his literacy skills, but without him becoming aware of this! The welfare support available for him was used to support him in lessons by writing down anything he needed from his dictation. Individual sessions were given over to writing a story. He worked with Simon, an 18-year-old ex-pupil who was waiting to go to ballet school. Together they wrote three books all emanating from an initial sequence in which Dean's mother won the pools. The whole family decides to go to Australia to visit relatives. Dean and Simon wrote letters and found books in the library in order to get the details correct. The timetables, maps, kinds of boats, etc. are accurately presented in a funny and fast-moving story. Dean added to his family members of the staff and the headmaster of the school, perhaps showing his gradual relaxation and acceptance of the school environment.

Dean's transfer to real reading occurred when he wanted to write about surfing and found he didn't know enough about it. I casually asked whether I should write a bit for him. He agreed, and at the next session I produced a text in which he rides the biggest of all surf waves in order to teach his friend how to do it (see p. 43). He rides in to the cheers of the people on the beach. Dean's amusement and pleasure at finding himself the hero in the story quite overcame his reluctance to read. At the end, when he was told how well he was reading, he was surprised. He had learned to put into operation the reading strategies that teachers had been trying to teach him for six years. His gradual long-term improvement in confidence and use of his undoubted ability meant that he achieved a reasonable grade in English in his GCSE leaving examinations.

Finding new materials that meet the needs of such unconfident and distressed readers is often very difficult. Conventional texts are too obviously babyish, remedial or else too difficult. A tailor-made text, taking little time and able to be scribed by a helper, can mean that a boy like Dean has a new start, a new way of regaining confidence and having success in an area formerly of great anxiety.

USING DICTATED STORIES WITH DYSLEXIC CHILDREN

Has this approach anything to offer children who are bright and articulate but defeated by their inability to read and write? All good reading and writing experiences will benefit all children. Because dictating stories over-arches the performative side of writing, it is particularly helpful to children who may be very frustrated by their inability to get down all that they want to communicate. Having a model of how your story should look is helpful – the often excellent verbal creativity of such writers is given recognition and their use of words validated. Using the words from a writer's own story as the basis for a spelling programme can reawaken interest and provide the beginning of a real writing vocabulary for the things that the writer really wants to say.

There is provision for the use of an amanuensis (our familiar scribe) at all levels up to University degree level. A well-planned programme of spelling and handwriting can be built on reading texts created by the readers themselves. These practise real reading skills and generalisation can be gradually introduced to increase the writing vocabulary. It is often a long and arduous progress but the computer with built-in spell check is the key to progress at later levels of education. By using such a writer's own words and ideas their intelligence and creativity is given validity and this can reverse the negative image which such children (and some teachers) have of their abilities.

For children of all ages and all abilities the dictated text can be the bridge for them into literacy. For some children this enabling bridge will quickly give them the confidence in themselves as readers and writers to encourage them to take on the task for themselves. For others, understanding the communicative function of written texts, both as a reader and as an author, is the crucial understanding which enables them to see the point of learning to read.

Other children may never be fully able to realise their communicative ability and find a way of communicating their feelings and understandings without some kind of help. It is essential, though, that help is given to allow them to express their feelings and to communicate their thoughts. Stories allow children to engage with meaning at a deep and important level and they provide important reading matter not only for the author but also for other children. Able learners who experience continued difficulty with reading and writing need the outlet of story and individual expression whilst they slowly learn to read and write.

WRITING BOOKS FOR BEGINNING READERS

Making up time for older readers who have missed out on early reading texts can be done by initiatives in secondary schools where books are written for younger children (Figure 20). In order to do this, extensive research into picture books and story books for younger children must be undertaken – in this way the toughest 14 year old in the school was happy to be seen reading and rereading John Burningham's *Would you Rather* because it was a resource for his work.

As a module at year 9 or 10 the process shown in Figure 20 can be a very supportive and adult way of reinforcing reading skills and practising reading and writing. It gives incidental but important messages about reading to small children and the kinds of books they like. We included a visit to a children's bookshop and the library quite deliberately

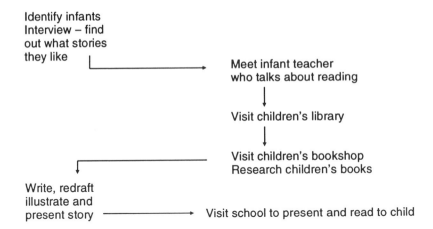

Identify infants
Interview – find
out what stories
they like

Meet infant teacher
who talks about reading

Visit children's library

Visit children's bookshop
Research children's books

Write, redraft
illustrate and
present story

Visit school to present and read to child

Figure 20 The process of writing books for infants

in the hope that it would be remembered by some of the pupils as a good place to take children when they were parents themselves.

CAN'T TELL A STORY, CAN'T REMEMBER IT!

Some teachers have reported that some children 'have no story to tell' and that they have not been able to compose a book. Other teachers have said that they have tried making a book with children with severe difficulties and that the children have enjoyed the process but that they have not been able to read the book when it is printed.

These points can perhaps be clarified in a brief way, although when it comes down to actual practice, the experience of matching ways into the process will vary for each individual child.

No stories to tell

This syndrome is quite common with children who are in retreat from the whole process of reading. In the research sample Darren was sulky and uncooperative on one occasion. He had told all his stories and there was an impasse. It would probably have been better to leave composing for the session and read together or play a game, but the helper was over-anxious about completing the task. In discussion it was suggested that she get Darren to talk about something he was interested in and then when he expressed something well, write it down, read it back to him, and suggest that it had the elements of a text in it. In this way his story of his holiday in Devon was written – it is actually the most mature and syntactically advanced of all his stories. Justine was bored with the idea of stories until she communicated the excitement of being a bridesmaid and *My Sister's Wedding*, with its sequels of *My Auntie's Baby* and *My Sister's Baby*, was started.

Often children who are reluctant or feel they have no story to tell have no sense that there is a story in them. Gordon (11) stated that he wanted to learn to read so that "I will be a real person, be like everybody else." There actually seemed very little to celebrate in Gordon's life and it was hard to find out what he was interested in. In the end it turned out that he wanted to be a lorry driver and that he knew a very little about articulated lorries. Together we composed a story in which I put Gordon as the leader of a team of articulated lorry drivers taking a long inter-continental trip. On the way Gordon saved lives, rescued lorries whose brakes failed, found the way through impenetrable mountains and many other heroic deeds. I always had to suggest the scenario, but once it was started Gordon cheerfully expanded on the details. This emphasis on competence, ingenuity and success is often important for composers who may feel incompetent and defeated in the school context. Encouraging the 'narrator as competent' role can be a very good experience for some children. Using photographs of trips and school activities, taking photographs of the composers and asking them to bring in photographs can all stimulate stories. Once a story has been written and read, or sometimes once even a chapter has been written and read, then the composer's confidence often seems to grow.

Starting points for stories

- Photographs – a walk around the school grounds, in the park, in the playing area. (Polaroid is wonderful because it is immediate.)
- Drawings done by the composer.
- Drawings or illustrations cut out of a book.
- School activities.
- Story of my life.
- Stories based on interests.
- Stories in which it is possible to put the child as hero – this can sometimes be done by suggesting that the hero of the story has their own name. The *Rolls Royce Robber Mystery* (p. 1) was solved by John, the Genius Detective!
- Journeys can again be helpful – into space, underwater. Keith wrote a long book based around the AA book of maps. He and his helper would choose a route, talk about it and maybe find out what it looked like by consulting books, and then write a story of a journey through it.
- John, looking at photographs of a holiday I had in Scotland, wrote a

story about a car rally that went through the Scottish mountains which
included an Ordnance Survey map.
- Books about toys – Big Foot, Playmobil people, Lego constructions,
  seem to help some children to get started. Big Foot – a kind of remote
  control vehicle – actually acquired a wife and family in Stephen's
  story!

Children who can't read back

Danny couldn't get very far with *Batman and the Robbers* (see p. 77) because
he was really completely confused about what story it was he was trying
to tell. In contrast the step-by-step bicycle ride was a clear progression in
his head. He was taking the familiar ride as he told it to be written down.
This resulted in his being able to read the text when it was returned to
him, whereas he appeared to be quite unable to read back initially.

Jeffrey (see p. 44) could remember the story of a school trip and read it
back; although his ability to remember letters, even in his own name, was
variable from day to day, he could remember this story and read it out
easily. Reading many times, pointing to the words, is replicating the
activity perceived by Clarke to be the way in which young children teach
themselves to read before school.

On some occasions when difficulties have been reported it has been
found that some element of the process of composing and scribing has
been changed. Maybe the scribe has tape recorded the story rather than
writing it down, or they have changed the words or word order to a better
text. Sometimes too much has been dictated at one session and that
creates difficulties in rereading.

The speed of writing down, watching the words being written, is an
essential part of the process. Some scribes do this directly onto a computer so
that a print-out is available immediately, and because the children are
watching the letters appear on the screen this seems to work satisfactorily.

No words should be changed. If they are unacceptable – swear words
or words that you wouldn't want in a story – then that has to be negotiated by the scribe as the writing takes place. Remember Andrew's '?' in
his story. It is fine to say "I don't want to write that" or "I don't think the
teacher would like that" or "We don't put that sort of thing in a book". If
it is 'bad grammar' then it has to be remembered that this is a bridge text
from oral to written language and that the retention of familiar language
patterns may be one of the reasons that children can read back their own
stories. Editing work, although this often comes only at a later stage
because composers are pleased and satisfied with their early productions,
often encourages the composer to recognise and change such grammatical constructions.

Dialect, in all its forms, is likely to be an integral part of some children's stories. If there is a good input of stories read to the composer then they will eventually internalise a model of standard written English. If books are going to become part of the class library then it may be necessary to negotiate about the library copy and suggest that some changes could be made. This is like typing out a piece of emergent writing for public display so that the audience can read it and the writer has an example of how it looks whilst retaining the original and celebrating the writer's creativity.

Other ways of supporting a composer with difficulty reading back

Tape record the story. Read it slowly on the tape unless you have a tape recorder with a variable speed. The writer should listen with earphones and point to each word as it is read.

Repeated listening allows the writer to join in with the tape.

Increase the speed eventually (if possible) and reduce the volume to the point where the reader is dominant. (This is a brief version of Carol Chomsky's useful approach.)

Do shared reading for as long as necessary. Many children may need repeated and frequent sharings.

Teach the vocabulary of the story so that the composer can write the words. What you can write you can read and for some children this is a better and more positive way into reading.

Rewrite the text in different ways – as cartoon, with picture (rebus) support. Start with simple drawings with labels. Put the labels onto the drawing, learn to write the words, use the words in different ways.

COLLABORATIVE USE OF THE LANGUAGE EXPERIENCE APPROACH TO READING

There are many ways in which groups of children and an adult can collaborate together to make dictated stories (Figure 21). The use of these stories can be varied. The story is composed collaboratively in the group and is written down by the helper. The common story is printed out and given back to each child to make the kinds of changes, illustrations, insertions, etc. that will make the story their own individual effort. There are many possible outcomes from this basic activity.

Second year infants

A group of Year Two infants made a collaborative story for the Reception class. It was nearly Christmas and they thought the Reception class would like a story about Father Christmas. The ride in the hot air balloon allowed all the children to contribute.

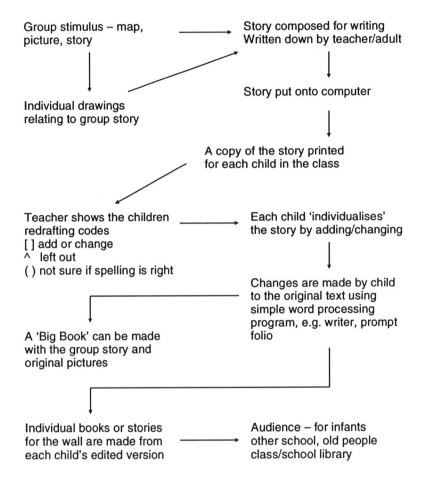

Figure 21 Collaborative ways of using the Language Experience approach to reading

The wind blew and blew.
They were cold.
The balloon moved sideways.
The ballon went down.
They were on the ground in Christmas land.
It was snowing.

Next a part of the story was given to each child to illustrate. While they were doing this the story itself was typed onto the computer, and then read together several times. The main version was cut up, linked to a picture and stuck into a big book.

At a subsequent session every child was given a copy of the main story. We talked about changes and endings. Every child then made changes or added endings – some requiring to be scribed. They then made their own small book, illustrating, cutting and pasting texts and making a cover.

Language elements covered in this activity

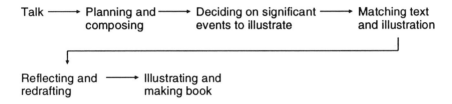

Figure 22 Language element in Year Two activity

Throughout this whole activity there is a significant amount of re-reading of text being done. Repetition of familiar words is practised but in a meaningful and relevant context. Words are remembered and often written down because they are needed.

Junior class (Year 5 and 6) in a school for children with moderate learning difficulties

A shared enterprise with the class teacher and welfare assistant enabled each child in the class to write their own story. Danny (p. 78) was one of these children.

As well as motivating and encouraging reading in the class there was a need to introduce the notion of writing as a process and to set up structures for supporting writing in the classroom. The process included those aspects shown in Figure 23.

Leavers' class in a school for children with moderate learning difficulties

This class had a day of working on making a book for the infant class. Their teacher felt that much of the work that they did was necessarily pragmatic and practical – relating to the skills for living that they were going to need when they left school. In order to reaffirm the importance of story, a day was given over to this shared activity. The process followed the usual pattern for group scribed writing but the illustration of the book and the need to reiterate ideas through talking was given more prominence.

Shared story making.

↓

The great hot air balloon – an unfinished story of the class in Space!

↓

Drawings were made to illustrate the story.

↓

Each member of the class had a copy of the story.

↓

An introduction to redrafting was given on the blackboard.

↓

Learning spellings by using the Look, Cover, Write, Check strategy was introduced.

↓

Each writer made their own reminder sheet.
They practised the spelling strategy by learning each of the stages as they wrote them down. (Danny proved to have a fast and accurate visual memory – his way into reading was going to be through writing.) (See Danny's prompt sheet in Figure 24.)
The children who found it most difficult were also introduced to the idea of tracing the word with a finger whilst saying it as an interim stage in learning to write it correctly.

↓

They were encouraged to change or add to the main text. Examples of their changes reflect the way in which they want to impress their own character on the joint writing.
Stephen's changes in Figure 25 show his wish to add a little more robustness to the story!

↓

Individual endings to the story were made. Some children wrote their own. Some were scribed for them.

↓

They were made into simple books.

↓

They read each other's books – in this way they repeated the text many times but there were differences, even if they were small between the texts and they had to concentrate to be able to read the different parts.

↓

Some children tape recorded their story.
A tape cover was designed.
Tape and book were kept in a plastic zip folder and the reading resources of the classroom were increased.

Figure 23 The process of composing the hot air balloon story

First we talked about favourite stories, stories they had enjoyed as children, and tried to identify what they had liked. Pictures came high on

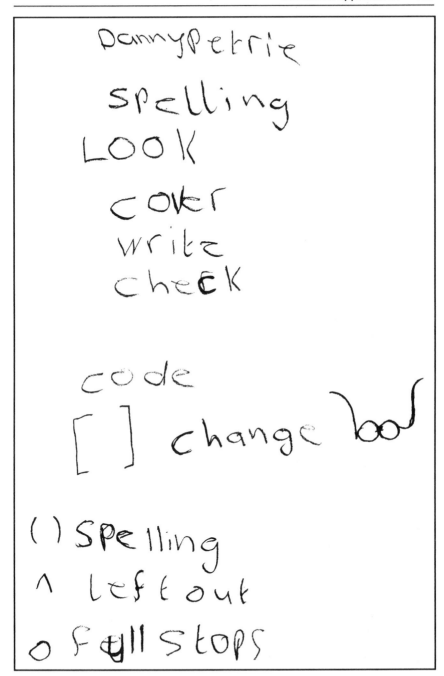

Figure 24 Danny's prompt sheet

Once upon a time we were all
in a hot air balloon.
We were travelling for
thousands and thousands of
miles.
We all went to sleep for half
a day and when we woke up

Stephen
↓
[Lee] looked over one side. His
eyes nearly popped out of his
head.
He saw a rough ground it was
stoney and really hot.
There was a plain red sky
with purple clouds with faces
on them. Flying in the sky was

the [flying horse.] It was   *a flying kangaroo*
orange with a red tail and   *and a flying dustBin*
red mane. It had big silver   *lorry*
wings. Katherine heard music
and the flapping of wings.] The
balloon floated down gently   *out*
onto the green earth. [Lee] *stephen*
jumped out while the balloon

Figure 25 Stephen's changes to the story

the list. The title *The Teddy Bears' Picnic* was chosen by one of the class and developed around a journey that a family of bears took through the woods in order to have a picnic. They met a variety of hazards on the way – sinking sands, wolves at large and so on.

On this occasion, because the group was quite large (15) and some of them had severe difficulties with speech, communication and understanding, it was necessary to add further elements of clarification and organisation into the activity, as described in Figure 26.

All these approaches to reading, writing and spelling for children with very considerable difficulties were done through the medium of story and words that were meaningful and in which the children were intrinsically interested. The purpose of the activity was clearly to produce material which they, and others, would read with enjoyment and intention.

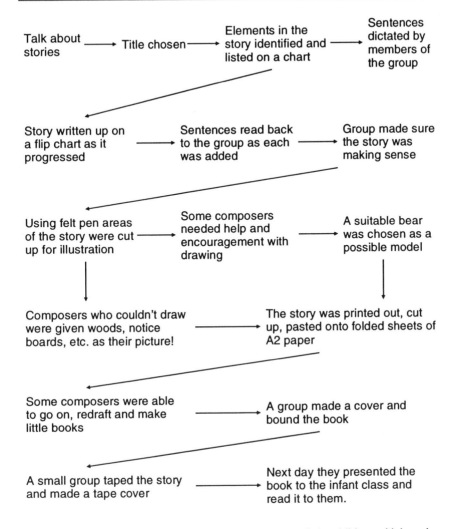

Figure 26 The process of composing a group story made by children with learning difficulties

Some learners who have repeatedly failed on conventional remedial materials very quickly show that they too need the power of story in order to find their way into reading and writing.

LEARNING TO READ IN A CULTURAL CONTEXT

If the effectiveness of learning to read through your own stories is predicated on the importance of starting with the learner's own language, then there are obvious benefits for learners whose cultural, and some-times language, needs are not met by conventional books.

Work with traveller children

This population of children often respond best to a validation of their own stories. The cultural context and interest in their own history is rarely found in printed books and yet story is an integral part of traveller culture and many travellers bring a wealth of story telling experience to their literacy learning. If teachers ignore this they have to start teaching language in a form and context that is unfamiliar and where progress is likely to be very slow.

Traveller children want to read quickly, seeing it as one of the valid activities in school. They often have good memories and visual acuity which means they often 'remember' the story very quickly, only gradu-ally differentiating the individual words. They are, however, 'reading' in an experiential way and they gain confidence and encouragement from a feeling of being able to read quickly. Many excellent dictated books are made by traveller education units. These should be on the shelves of all school libraries and they provide good ideas and inspiration for other stories. In the example in Figure 27 the 'told' quality of the story has been kept but put into conventional print and standard English.

Books can be simple or elaborate and should be shared with others as well as being on the bookshelf as a visible sign of the children's own culture. Teachers might need to be aware of cultural taboos on certain subjects or words – but if they are guided by the child's own ideas then they are unlikely to get into difficulties. Traveller support teachers can often be very helpful here. Sometimes children are told not to talk about their home life in school and this should be respected; on the other hand one boy wrote numerous stories about squirrels in which it did seem that the life and happenings in the squirrel's family closely mirrored his own! Most children though enjoy seeing stories about their own lives in print. Ernie (8) wrote about his dog:

> *She plays with the footballs and makes me laugh. She bites with her little teeth. My puppy has got a new kennel outside round the back. She has got a long chain and a little tail. She is black and brown and her shape is like a horse. She is tall as a cat and the cat is smaller than Pickwick. Pickwick is Leonard's dog used for coursing.*

This story about a dog is likely to be more motivating for Ernie to read than a story about a dog curled up in a basket in front of a fire in a house. Travellers who gain confidence in school may produce books that include Romany vocabulary. These are good resources for Knowledge about

Stoves in the waggon times were well known in the waggon, but my Grandmother used to cook outside in an eight gallon cast iron boiler. She could put a turkey in one at Christmas times and put it over a stick fire, or next to a stick fire and it would roast and roast until it was golden brown and beautifully cooked.

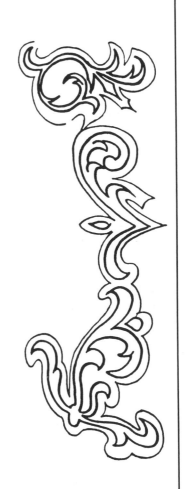

Figure 27 An extract from a story dictated by a traveller child

Language work and provide a further legitimisation of traveller culture which is badly needed.

Dual language stories

Much of the initial work with dual language stories was the result of encouraging adults to tell stories from their own culture and then getting written translations and illustrations to make proper books. This still seems an excellent way into English for many children. It is necessary to find a competent English speaker who can translate – but there is often a relative who can do this for the child at home if there is no language support service available.

An Israeli boy arriving in England with no English was in a mono-lingual class. He wrote many books in Hebrew which his father translated for him at home. The teacher made the dual language books, illustrated by the boy, into a classroom feature. Her English children were fascinated by seeing Hebrew written down, the boy was writing at his own level of conceptual development but being provided with the scaffolding for learning English. Many aspects of other languages can be used to interest and inform all the children in a class.

Making books in which all learners' languages are represented helps mono-lingual children to widen their language experience and to gain an understanding of other cultures and of their own language.

Dual language dictated stories placed on the same page and illustrated with the author's own pictures can be made into classroom books for all the children to read. Using a format such as 'Would you be scared . . .?', and adding the children's answers in all the classroom languages, introduces children to more formal English structures whilst retaining their own involvement (Figure 28).

Some possible ways of creating dual language books are shown in Figure 29. For the children who can speak, but not write, their mother tongue, a process is outlined in Figure 30, whilst Figure 31 concerns those children who are able to write their mother tongue.

There are many ways forward into literacy but the dictated story, starting with the learner's own needs and language capacities, can prove to be the most influential and solid base on which further literacy skills can be built.

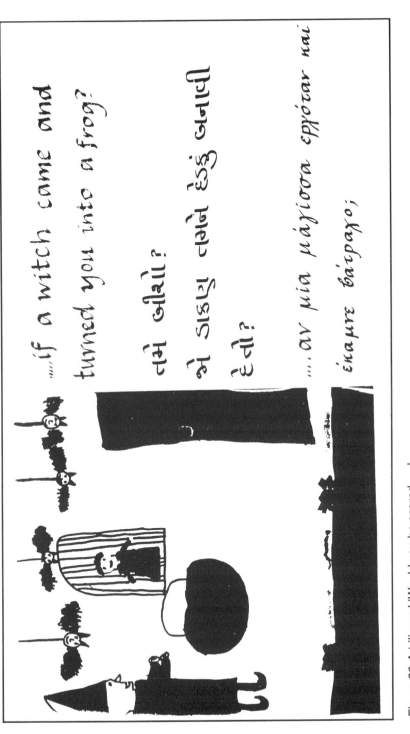

Figure 28 A trilingual 'Would you be scared . . .'

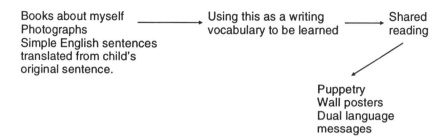

Figure 29 Possible ways of creating dual language books.

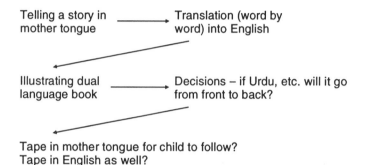

Figure 30 Creating a book with a child who speaks but does not write the mother tongue

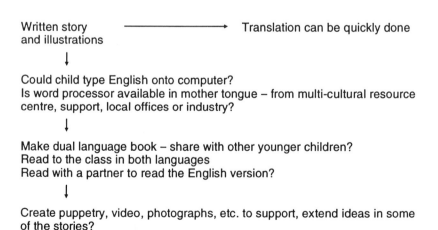

Figure 31 Creating a book with a child who can write the mother tongue

Chapter 7

Ways forward

Maintaining progress and progressing into other aspects of literacy

Children who are in the process of becoming fluent readers and who enjoy books, stories and expressing their own feelings and ideas can find a great deal of pleasure in seeing their ideas and pictures transformed into a reading text. Ruth (7) is the sister of Sam (pp. 91–2). The work with Sam was intended to help him at all levels to express his ideas and to understand what a book was and how it came to be written. Ruth, skilled at drawing and on the threshold of successful reading, also wanted to make a book.

It is obvious from the illustrations and the examples of the text shown in Figure 32 that here is a child engaged in composing in a serious and purposeful way. Here the 'common ground' between reader and author is made explicit in action; here the notions of cohesion, interest and language combine in a text which shows the internalisation of 'book' language and literary conventions. Children do not grow out of dictated stories, they transform them into more complex stories and they use them to try out their newly acquired book knowledge.

THE MAINTENANCE OF READING

The problem with work with many readers, particularly older readers, is that without continual practice reading skills can be lost again. Initial work with dictated stories can precipitate reading but there has to be, particularly for less able pupils, long-term support if they are going to retain the ability to read. The emphasis on encouraging volunteer helpers who would be prepared to work with an individual or small group of children over a period of time is to avoid the danger of this becoming a 'one off' activity. Although making a book is motivating and can increase a reader's confidence and give practice in reading skills it is rarely sufficient to depend on one text to effect real changes.

The gradual transfer to other conventional texts is essential if progress is going to be maintained. The amount of sustained reading which is essential for secondary pupils is sometimes minimal, reading is often short-burst, highly condensed and subject-vocabulary type, and this is

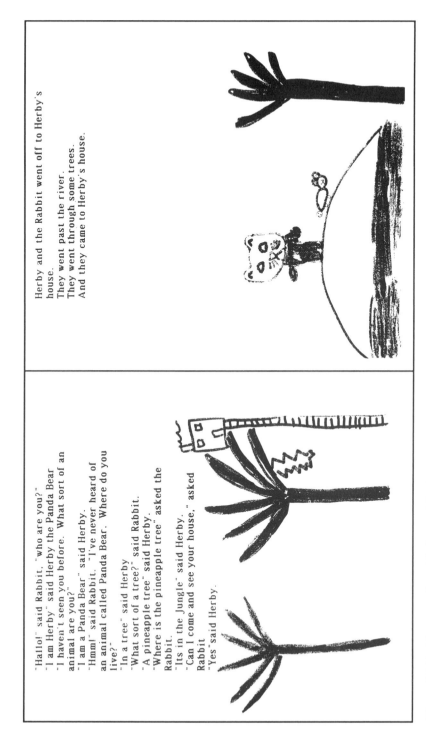

"Hallo!" said Rabbit, "who are you?"
"I am Herby" said Herby the Panda Bear
"I haven't seen you before. What sort of an animal are you?"
"I am a Panda Bear" said Herby.
"Hmm!" said Rabbit. "I've never heard of an animal called Panda Bear. Where do you live?"
"In a tree" said Herby
"What sort of a tree?" said Rabbit.
"A pineapple tree" said Herby.
"Where is the pineapple tree" asked the Rabbit.
"Its in the Jungle" said Herby.
"Can I come and see your house," asked Rabbit
"Yes" said Herby.

Herby and the Rabbit went off to Herby's house.
They went past the river.
They went through some trees.
And they came to Herby's house.

Figure 32 Ruth's story about Herby and the Rabbit

material which is too difficult for the emerging reader and which merely repeats earlier failure. Transfer and further materials are therefore crucially important for continued improvement.

Some ways of supporting reading after the initial stages

In-class reading needs to be supported by *helpers* who will *scribe* notes, information and other class material for pupils.

Tapes can be made of material which is to be needed for reading and then pupils can use the tape either in class or at home. (Some schools use Walkmans for these.)

At all stages a *range of reading texts* for any particular subjects is needed. This needs to include well-illustrated texts where pictures and diagrams support the reading. Using dictated texts in the field of information – maybe texts dictated to be used by others in the class or by younger children – can be one way of retaining impetus and maintaining practice.

The encouragement of *shared reading* between pupils where a better reader reads with, or sub-vocalises for, a less proficient reader.

Sometimes transfer may be to *magazines, newspapers or comics* rather than books. Here the language is often simpler and more predictable and in the case of comics is supported by pictures carrying the same meaning.

Computer programs demand considerable reading and they have a built-in correction system – if you don't read it right then you don't succeed. Shared reading in following instructions and working through problems is helpful. Special educational adventure games contain a lot of predictable and supported reading material and pupils are highly motivated to read it correctly.

Recipes can be useful. Less nutritionally valuable in the food sense but very helpful for literacy are the 'instant' packet foods that have instructions supported by diagrams on the back.

Tapes of stories with the text to read alongside can be a very helpful and private way of practising reading skills. If the story is interesting enough the reader can be encouraged to read it many times, first following the words with a finger, then gradually joining in. The volume on the tape recorder can be turned down as proficiency increases but the support is there if needed.

Poetry is often short, supported sometimes by rhymes, and has an internal rhythm that is engaging and can carry readers into the magic of words. It is certainly not too difficult for less experienced readers – in fact in a short space it often conveys a depth of meaning and understanding that speaks very much to less confident readers' condition.

An interested and enthusiastic adult who reads to children will automatically interest children in reading for themselves. If that enthusiasm is generated by the teacher reading stories, poems and interesting information books and talking about them with the class then all children will want to join the 'reading club'.[1] With those who are older maybe we have to be less elitist in our aspirations and accept that interest in teenage magazines, words of pop songs or fanzine publications may interest Justine more than proper books. Newspapers, sports reports and fishing and computer journals are also popular but do not necessarily figure in the class or school library or in individual reading sessions. Younger children need their teachers to know their book stock well enough to be able to match their reading needs or to provide stimulating and interesting material that is either taped or shared with another reader. A wide range of different kinds of dictated texts can be produced to meet the different needs of learners. It is the very individual nature of the dictated story, meeting both the linguistic and the psychological needs of the learner, that makes it a powerful tool for learning to be a competent reader.

Involving parents can help a great deal – particularly if they can type or are prepared to write down homework, stories or make books with the children at home. Bilingual children can often be helped by elder brothers or sisters who can act as translators of familiar stories or family happenings. Making bilingual books can also help sustain the mother tongue language. Mary made a dual language French/English translation of the book her group had written. The time-consuming dictation, printing and rereading can often be done by a volunteer helper. The skill of the classroom teacher or the learning support teacher comes in using the texts, extending activities from them, ensuring that the necessary secretarial skills of writing are learned and that the strategies for reading are gradually generalised.

It is not just being able to read aloud correctly that constitutes effective reading; it is the ability to understand, to recall, make inferences and apply knowledge acquired through the text that is necessary. The experience of composing with a scribe is the foundation, for most learners, of practising and understanding the necessary skills involved in writing and communicating effectively.

READING AND READING COMPREHENSION

As with other aspects of learning to read it is the generalisation of the learning that gradually builds up to a repertoire of reading skills that are effective and incremental. Lack of motivation has been seen as one of the ways in which reading failure is perpetuated. The negative and passive response to texts makes the practice of reading almost impossible. The 'word by word' reading of texts that are not intrinsically interesting means poor recall and insufficient understanding.

All the usual ways in which teachers support comprehension of a text can be used with a dictated text. A range of activities relating to Ian's story, *The Andorra Truck Mystery*, was undertaken not just by Ian but by the small group with whom he was working. This gave material for:

Discussion work
Drama
Writing
Prediction of the end of the story
Close reading and comprehension

Other ways of working on and mediating text can relate to making a script for a broadcast, retelling through acting or puppetry, producing additional materials – tapes, pictures for the wall, video, etc. (as shown in Figure 33). Using the story with younger children can often be an important way of understanding it further.

Because the material used is 'owned' by the author, the language is predictable and they can read it successfully, these common comprehension-type activities can be undertaken sooner than would be possible if printed texts were used. Learners therefore begin to internalise the strategies for comprehension and the need for reflection from the beginning of their reading practice.

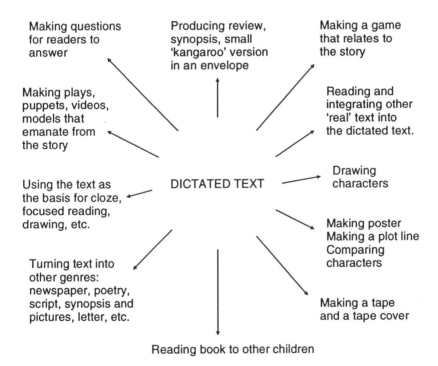

Figure 33 Activities related to a dictated text

EXTENDING WRITING ACTIVITIES

Once the initial text is completed there are a lot of additional activities that can arise from it which will reinforce the secretarial aspects of writing and increase the opportunities for composers to try out their ideas by writing independently.

For very young or very slowly progressing writers it can be helpful to transform their dictated text into a Breakthrough activity. Conventional Breakthrough folders and cards can be used or a simple version can be made inside the back cover of the dictated book (see Figure 34).

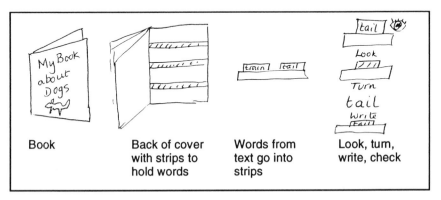

| Book | Back of cover with strips to hold words | Words from text go into strips | Look, turn, write, check |

Figure 34 Turning dictated text into a Breakthrough activity

Activities like Breakthrough, in which the words from the text are presented to the reader individually to use for reading and writing, help to concentrate attention on the words and letters. With older pupils such words can be subject-based words and can be supported by other activities such as Tray or Cloze Comprehension programs on the computer.

SPELLING – LEARNING THE SECRETARIAL SKILLS OF WRITING

It is essential that a good spelling and handwriting programme underpin the language learning which is taking place in the composing and reading of dictated stories. However, there is considerable evidence to show that lists of words are difficult to learn, and that they do not easily generalise to other vocabulary. The dictated story gives the teacher the key to the words that the writer wants to learn to spell. Words that are important from the text, and generalisations from those words, can be the basis for a learned writing vocabulary. These are words in the composer's latent written vocabulary that they know how to use, and want to use, and they are therefore optimally ready to learn how to spell them.

Jeffrey's dictated story about his bike sets the agenda for a spelling programme. He writes:

I bought a mountain bike second hand. I'm going to strip it down and build it up again. It is not very good. It has got a puncture in the front and only one brake. The gear slips and the seat slants. I've bought two tins of paint red and blue. I'm going to spray it.

From this passage the words are identified that he is interested in and then analogies are made that relate to the look of the word, not the sound of the word, and he is taught the strategy of looking at each word, covering it up, writing it and checking so that he can learn the key vocabulary for himself.

gear	mountain	bike	paint	spray
ear	fountain	like	mountain	day
heart	round	spike	rain	play
earth				
fear				

Spelling should be initiated in a positive, light-hearted way and there should be no possibility of failure. The following procedure covers the stages needed for learning new words.

Take each word that the composer has chosen to learn to spell, look carefully and discuss how it LOOKS and similar words or words within the word that LOOK the SAME even if they do not sound the same.

Figure 35 Gary's work showing the LOOK, COVER, WRITE, CHECK process

Encourage the composer to LOOK at the word, COVER the word up, WRITE the word, CHECK if it is right (Figure 35). Have another go if it is not correct.

Word lists can be put in the back of stories but it is often best to keep the secretarial aspects of writing as a separate activity.

A book can build up into a compendium of related games, word lists, independent writing, etc. (Figure 36), and many children who have experienced failure will enjoy compiling such evidences of their increasing abilities.

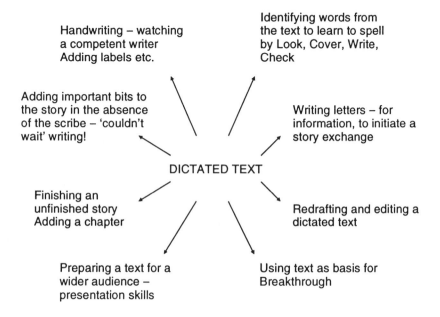

Handwriting – watching a competent writer Adding labels etc.

Identifying words from the text to learn to spell by Look, Cover, Write, Check

Adding important bits to the story in the absence of the scribe – 'couldn't wait' writing!

Writing letters – for information, to initiate a story exchange

DICTATED TEXT

Finishing an unfinished story Adding a chapter

Redrafting and editing a dictated text

Preparing a text for a wider audience – presentation skills

Using text as basis for Breakthrough

Figure 36 Some additional ways of using a dictated text to support writing

DICTATED INFORMATION TEXTS

Texts that support topic work in the classroom are often too difficult for beginning readers. Work using these books, even with more proficient readers, is often identified as being copying without real understanding. As schools begin to build up resources related to topic areas in the National Curriculum they could consider adding dictated texts to each of the topic resource boxes. In this way purposeful research and composing has a real audience in readers who would otherwise find topic books too difficult.

Although this kind of activity is time consuming it is possible that volunteer helpers could undertake it or that it would be a very valuable way of using support teachers or auxiliaries in the classroom. Support teachers, with their specialist knowledge of language and texts, would be able to make study skills and information books relevant in a new way to their individual or groups of learners.

Reading and writing supported by composing dictated information texts

- Collecting together and reading relevant texts with scribe.
- Learning study skills – contents, indexing, skimming, scanning.
- Shared reading that reinforces these skills.
- Deciding on chapters – planning content.
- Dictating information text .
- Providing suitable illustrations that are labelled.
- Giving a contents and index page.

Support materials that could be included in the activity

- Tape
- Tape plus slides (made from blank slides using OHP pens) to give a tape/slide show to the class
- Poster advertising book
- Broadcast reading parts of the book and talking about how it was made.

Included in the reading and writing activities are valuable Knowledge about Language possibilities for reflecting on different registers in text, organisation, use of language, specialist vocabulary, etc. (see Figure 37).

THE RELEVANCE OF THE LANGUAGE EXPERIENCE APPROACH TO RECOVERY PROGRAMMES

Teachers are currently aware of many 'recovery' approaches to literacy and the pressures to conform to particular methods or ways of approaching reading. Reports have indicated though that an eclectic approach which takes account of the learners' own capabilities, needs and intentions works best. The Language Experience approach exemplifies all of these aspects of literacy teaching.

It is possible to combine this active approach to learning to read and write with the development of phonological awareness in writing through encouraging the reader's own emergent writing and, particularly where the learner is older, by a carefully implemented spelling programme based on the learning of an effective strategy.[2] The intensive support of reading and writing through the Clay Reading Recovery Programme[3] includes within it the use of familiar and frequently read texts and the

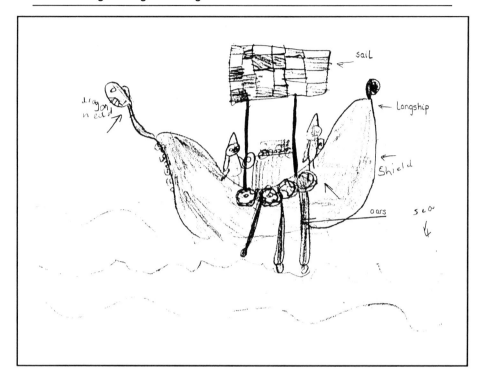

VIKING BOATS

Vikings used their longships to get
treasure and sell things to other
people. They used sails when it was
windy. When it was not windy, they
used oars to row.

The dragonhead at the front of the boat
scared people away as the Vikings came
towards them. The shields stopped the
Vikings getting hurt when they were
fighting. They fought to get gold and
treasure and sometimes they took
animals too.

Figure 37 Part of Kay's text on Vikings, and accompanying picture

encouragement of children's own writing by scribing for them. Clay reinforces the importance of the reciprocity between reading and writing and the acknowledgement of the developmental nature of early writing. The approach suggested in this present book has, in common with such programmes, an emphasis on active learning, beginning with the learner's own language capabilities, a structured and evaluative approach from the teacher and consistent and on-going support for the learner. The dictated text is a bridge text. What it is doing is 'unfreezing' formal written text and giving it a voice, the composer's own voice, that is heard on the page. It makes explicit the implicit strategies for reading and writing and encourages the practice of real, relevant and meaningful reading and writing skills in a positive and engaged way. For both participants in the activity it is an interesting, motivating and important enterprise.

Chapter 8

Assessment and evaluation

This reading/writing activity is so useful partly because it includes all areas of language. Generated in oral language it allows the composer to try out all kinds of aspects of writing in a safe and supported way. The reading of the finished text practises real reading skills and the text can be used for reading comprehension work, as a resource for learning spellings and as a springboard for other language activities.

Quantifying such achievements is not simple, although aspects of competence identified in the National Curriculum in England and Wales can certainly be seen to be covered and accordingly assessed. In areas where the National Curriculum criteria are not of relevance there are likely to be other language policies or curricula which cover the same kind of ground.

What is possible is a criterion-referenced approach in which necessary experiences and learning are evaluated against the experience and learning of the composers/readers themselves. In this way progress can clearly be seen. Self-evaluation and the qualitative evaluation of the helpers can also be made evident.

Some researchers have suggested that dictated stories can give us other measures of language development and these are also considered.

ASPECTS OF THE LANGUAGE CURRICULUM (INCLUDING N.C. ENGLISH FOR ENGLAND AND WALES) WHICH ARE COVERED BY COMPOSING AND READING DICTATED TEXTS

Talking and listening (Figure 38)

Evaluating talk and listening is notably difficult. Artificial situations do not give teachers the data they require. The informal diary of the helper may contain indications of progress in this area and these can be noted and added into the child's oral language profile.

An informal interview between teacher and child, talking about the book they have made, would allow the teacher to cover all aspects of

Elements	Activity	Indications of progress
Talking to an interested adult Listening Responding appropriately Planning Sequencing a story Sequencing information Discussing changes to the text Asking questions Evaluating	Takes place in interactions during composing and reading Composing Editing Seeking clarification Talks about dictated text to teacher, to peers	Talks in a positive and relaxed way Concentrates and listens carefully 'Gets the message' Increased coherence in talking about things, e.g. news time, sharing Prepared to contribute to group discussion Talks more appropriately, i.e. is more to the point Asks questions that are relevant Listens to the answers

Figure 38 Talking and listening aspects

talking and listening. If the interview is tape recorded then the records can be filled in at a later date. As with reading it is intimidating for a child, or anyone for that matter, to be talking to someone who is making notes.

Writing (Figure 39)

Collecting and using the evidence

Interview

Talking about the dictated book with the composer will make evident progress in many of these areas. Again taping would be easier than trying to listen and to assess at the same time.

Interview with scribe, scribe diaries

Many helpers are able to describe coherently the kind of progress they feel that their composer has made. Some of these observations can be written in the helper's diary, but some non-professionals are more comfortable being able to talk.

Evidence from the text

As with the evaluation of written work, a folder containing photocopied

Elements	Activity	Indications of progress
Planning	Deciding on a story line	Planning diagrams, notes, drawings
Composing	Telling the story coherently	Story 'hangs together' The narrator's voice is consistent Tense is consistent Use of third person past tense where appropriate Contexts are defined Characters are defined
	Using written language	The story reads like a written story Sentences or clauses are subordinated Range of conjunctions begins to be used Vocabulary is wide Difference between dialogue and main text? Less colloquialisms, contractions, tenses not agreeing Changes are made
Reflecting Redrafting Presentation	Editing Sense of audience	Reasons are given for changes Knows appropriate 'book' features – title, author, etc. Can explain about the reader's needs

Figure 39 Writing aspects

evidence over a period of time is probably the most illuminating and useful way of evaluating progress.

Notes at intervals which commented on a piece of text might include the written text measures identified above, e.g. examples of new or un-expected vocabulary, examples of more complex use of sentences.

Helpers or teachers should try and keep scribed plans, notes indicating planning of the story.

Editing

This was found to be a cogent example of increased confidence on the part of the composer about what written text might be like. It was also a way of introducing the idea of redrafting and a redrafting code to the composer. The instructions to the helper in this area may be a helpful guide to teachers wanting to monitor this important aspect of progress.

Again tape recording made it possible for the teacher to have access to the actual process of editing taking place (as well as giving an example of reading back). Two print-outs of the text were given – one for the child to read and one for the helper to mark changes on.

1 Collect two copies of the last chapter from the tray.
2 Switch on the tape recorder.
3 Let the child read it back to you.
4 Note in pencil on the printed page any alterations the child wants to make, anything they want to put in or any mistakes in the printing they have found.
   Use this code to alter the text:
   ( )   spellings – misprints
   ^   left out
   O   punctuation
   [ ]   the bit I want to change, alter or add to
5 If they make few or no changes you could ask the following questions:
a. Is there anything that doesn't make sense?
b. Is there anything you could change so that it sounds more interesting?
c. Which bit do you like best? Do you want to add anything here?
   It would be helpful if you could ask why they want to make the change and make a note of the reason.

Teachers might want to note ways in which children, whilst they are acquiring writing skills, are showing evidence of understanding the use of language in writing and the way in which stories are constructed. It would be unlikely that a recording form such as that suggested below would be useful for large numbers of children but its use with a pupil who is being monitored closely for progress, or as a way for a teacher to look for further understanding of the underlying processes involved in composing it could prove to be useful. It is the eventual record that I found helpful in assessing progress in the composers in my research sample.

Name:
Age/class:
Title of story:
Planning (notes, helper's diary):

Vocabulary (words used that are unlikely to be in spoken vocabulary):

Use of conjunctions:
most sentences joined with *and*:

other conjunctions used:

Tenses: main tense used (present, simple past):

tense shifts, inconsistencies – frequent, infrequent:

Story structure
Sequence:
consistent sequence?
chronological?
containing flashforward and flashback?

Plot:
arising from characters?
arising from episodes?
inexplicit?
based on known story?
based on film or TV story?

Characters:
number?
significant names?
differentiated by description, actions, thought processes?

Closing procedures
ties up the ends? reprises?

The most valuable aspect of making or using such a detailed record is the way in which it focuses what is going on in the composition and gives the teacher insight into the learning that is taking place. The kind of informal assessment, informed by understanding of what constitutes progress, of the type shown in the Primary Language Record (CPLE) and containing actual evidence from the child's work, is probably, long term, the most helpful.

Recording spelling

It is important that spelling arising from dictated work is recorded and monitored so that the whole range of letter sequences is eventually taught to the child. Keeping some kind of record, on index cards or in a word book, helps the child to know what words and letter patterns they have learned. It also assists learning of spelling for individually based testing. The teacher also needs to have a record in order to make sure that a consistent learning agenda is being followed by pupils learning to be writers.

Name:
Age/class:
Title of story:
Key words (to use for generalising spelling patterns):

Generalisations taught:

Tested:

Reading

The progress in reading in the research was assessed by using mis-cue analysis. This gives a 'window' onto the process of reading and makes it possible to identify the cueing strategies that the reader is using. Tape recording all or some of the sessions of reading back – either with the helper or subsequently with the teacher – can give evidence for analysis of two important aspects of reading progress: changes in strategies over time and changes in independence. The value of tape recording is the way in which you can repeatedly listen. Recording Samantha's reading I had noted 'She has no phonic analysis strategies at all.' After listening several times to the tape I was able to hear a faint 'c.c.c.' in front of 'cooking' which made me revise my original assessment of what she knew about reading to include initial letter sound–letter correspondence.

Mis-cue analysis

Teachers are becoming increasingly familiar with mis-cue analysis and the way it gives an insight into the strategies that the child is using for reading. Substitutions, or mis-cues, can usually be seen to result from over-use of one strategy rather than using the range of strategies in order to read the text effectively. The number of self-corrections made by the reader is a valuable indication of improvement in reading for meaning and they should be noted. There are interesting and useful descriptions of the mis-cue analysis and its use in Arnold (1982) and Wray (1992) and a demonstration of its use is given in the BBC video *Teaching Reading* (1992). The Primary Language Record and many other language records and policies now contain suggestions for using this way of evaluating reading. As teachers become used to listening to children reading and assessing their use of strategies it is usually possible to do this in an informal way by just listening and noting tendencies towards strategies. This facility comes after more focused analysis has been undertaken.

Children can also do a simple mis-cue for themselves by listening to themselves reading and answering questions:

Does it make sense?
Is your reading jerky or smooth?
Does your reading sound interesting?
What do you do when you come to a word you can't read?

This can allow teachers to collect a tape of reading which the reader has also felt some sense of purpose in making and listening to. One boy remarked – "Of course if I got it not to be jerky then it would make sense and sound interesting." A valuable insight!

Task analysis

It has been found that analysis of the task can be one of the most useful supports for learners who may be experiencing difficulties. It focuses on the learning for the teacher, and it structures what is to be done for the learner, and encourages reflection and self-evaluation. Informal assessments of their own progress can be noted. The same process can be used with either the individual learner or the group engaged on a composing and reading activity. Each element of the task must be identified and an opportunity given for the learner to identify aspects of their own progress. This keeps learners on track of the task and also engages them actively in the process of their own learning. A possible self-evaluation form for a group dictated text activity is shown below

Activity: Group story
Group: Ian, John, Tracey, Sophie, Samantha
Choose title: *The Great Balloon Race*

Tell the story: Mrs. Archer wrote it for us

Draw picture: I drew a balloon and the landscape

Make a Big Book

Read the book
Get a print-out of the story. Do you want to make any changes?
                     I changed John to the pilot. I added a kangaroo.

Print in the changes
Draw picture
Make a small book

Read your book to a friend or teacher. Get them to put a comment about the book here:

Individual book making

The whole issue of diagnosis, improvement and learning programmes built on individual needs is of great importance if progress is to be clearly monitored and children are to acquire the necessary skills of literacy. The problem with older children who have failed, with defeated, passive or disturbed learners or those who have no confidence in their ultimate success is that it is often difficult to get sufficiently large samples of their work in order to analyse their needs. The output of many children when they are engaged in creating dictated stories is far greater than usual. They engage with writing and reading on a macro rather than a micro level and therefore teachers can more easily discern trends and potential growth points.

In the same way the text itself acts as a seedbed for remedial work that has relevance, importance and coherent meaning to the learner.

When this literacy activity is taken seriously, when the composer remains in control of their writing and the reader is taught to use all the strategies for reading, to self-correct and to make some evaluation of their own progress, then the dictated text becomes a powerful tool for learning and an important resource for the teacher for evaluating progress and planning potential development.

Appendix 1 Writing a book together

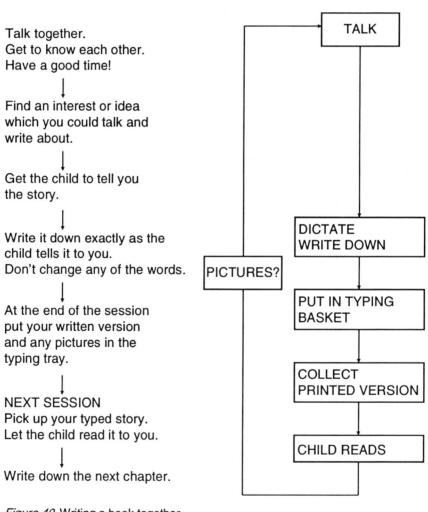

Talk together.
Get to know each other.
Have a good time!

↓

Find an interest or idea
which you could talk and
write about.

↓

Get the child to tell you
the story.

↓

Write it down exactly as the
child tells it to you.
Don't change any of the words.

↓

At the end of the session
put your written version
and any pictures in the
typing tray.

↓

NEXT SESSION
Pick up your typed story.
Let the child read it to you.

↓

Write down the next chapter.

TALK

PICTURES?

DICTATE
WRITE DOWN

PUT IN TYPING
BASKET

COLLECT
PRINTED VERSION

CHILD READS

Figure 40 Writing a book together

HOW TO BE A SCRIBE

This is an approach to helping children with reading difficulties.
The children use their own stories to help them to read.

Aims for readers and tutors

1 Enjoyment in writing and reading the stories.
2 Enjoyment in tutor and reader working together.
3 Improvement in reading skill.
4 The reader becomes more independent and begins to notice their own mistakes.
5 The reader begins to be critical of the way in which the story is written and to alter things where necessary.
6 The reader begins to transfer their skills to printed books.

How to start

1 Tell the child something about yourself and encourage them to talk to you about themselves and their interests.
2 Talk to the child about what you are going to do. Read to them or let them read one of the books which other children have written, or just look through the books together. See what ideas they have for a story. Jot down some notes if necessary. If it is difficult to find a topic to write about look at some pictures and see if they will give you any ideas.
3 Find a title.
4 Chapter One. The child dictates the story. If they get stuck ask questions or talk round the subject to help them to get going again.
   Write down what the child dictates on the paper. Let the child watch you write if they are interested so that they see how words are spelled and how a good writer writes.
   Encourage them to dictate in phrases or sentences rather than a word at a time.
   Write down exactly what the child says even if it is not good grammar or very well put. Sometimes when you read back to them what they have written they will want to change things.
5 When the flow of inspiration stops then it is time to suggest drawing pictures, finding pictures, illustrating a title page, or just talking about what you might add next time. Some children do not like to draw and finding pictures in magazines or even writing to somewhere for information could be a good idea. You could visit the school or local library or look through relevant books and magazines.

The reading back

1 Collect the book from the tray.
2 Let the child read it back to you. Correct as explained in the booklet (Appendix 2) – do too little correcting rather than too much. Be very positive and praise what the child has written.
3 Note in pencil on the printed page any alterations the child wants to make, anything they want to put in or any mistakes in the printing they have found.
4 Put the corrected sheet back in the typing tray if there is any work to be altered.

HELP!

What do I do if we get stuck?

Make a list of possible ideas. Look at some pictures. Talk about recent events, visits, etc.

If you are part way through a story stop and talk, look at books in the library. Allow the child to draw and talk about what they are drawing.

Make notes of what they say and any conversation that might relate to the story – often you will be able to start again using part of what the child has said.

Read a picture book together. They have no words and the child talks their way through the story by looking at pictures. There are many suitable books for all ages.

Do some reading together. A joke book is an 'easy' book to share. This allows you to read together – let the child read the bits they can – particularly the 'Knock Knock' jokes.

Read a story of their choice to the child. Let them join in, talk about the pictures, read short bits on their own if they wish.

HELPING THE TRANSFER TO ORDINARY BOOKS

This will be after the child has achieved considerable success with their own book. Please consult the teacher about the right time to introduce other writing unless it occurs naturally in the course of a session.

1 If the child is writing a book using factual material then 'write in' bits out of a book into their story.
2 Add a bit to the child's text – if they want it. For example, they may not know about something they want to put in their story – offer to write it in for them, or add another chapter. Ask the teacher to add a part of a chapter to the story. It is important that the child does not mind this.

3 Encourage children to look at books related to the subject, or pamphlets, leaflets, games, etc. are sometimes more acceptable.
4 Where appropriate encourage pupils to write or dictate letters to find out information. Read through replies with them.
5 Look for information sources – Yellow Pages, magazines, etc.
6 Some children may want to write down part of their story. Help them to do this. Encourage them to identify their own spelling mistakes after they have written them. Write the word down for them to look at. Cover it up. Let them write it. Check the spelling. Try again if it is wrong.
7 If chapters of the book are stored on disc there is a possibility of accessing the original from disc and the child editing or changing their original story actually on the screen.

EDITING

1 Collect two copies of the last chapter from the tray.
2 Switch on the tape recorder.
3 Let the child read it back to you.
4 Note in pencil on the printed page any alterations the child wants to make, anything they want to put in or any mistakes in the printing they have found.
   Use this code to alter the text:
   ( )   spellings – misprints
   ^   left out
   O   punctuation
   [ ]   the bit I want to change, alter or add to
5 If they make few or no changes you could ask the following questions:
a. Is there anything that doesn't make sense?
b. Is there anything you could change so that it sounds more interesting?
c. Which bit do you like best? Do you want to add anything here?
   It would be helpful if you could ask why they want to make the change and make a note of the reason.

Appendix 2   Reading a book together

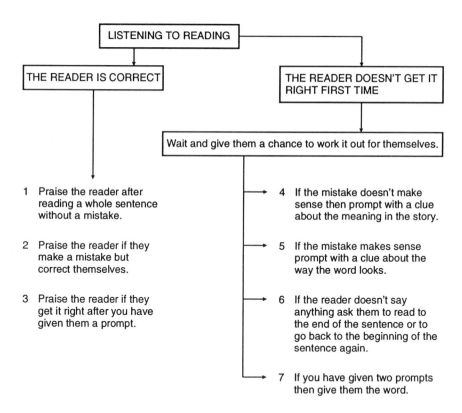

Figure 41 Reading a book together

1 *The reader is correct and reads a whole sentence without a mistake.*

Praise the reader. Just a quiet "Well done" or "Good" which doesn't interrupt the flow of the reading is all that is needed.

2 *The reader makes a mistake but corrects it themselves either immediately or after going on for a little way.*

Praise the child when they make the correction. If the mistake makes sense and the reader doesn't notice it allow them to continue but point out the mistake at the end of the reading.

3 *You have to prompt the reader but they then go back and correct the word.*

Praise the reader when they make the correction.

4 *If the mistake doesn't make sense.*

Ask a question about the meaning of the story.

5 *If the mistake makes sense.*

Draw attention to the way the word looks – its beginning and end.

6 *If the reader still doesn't say anything.*

Ask them to look ahead and see what is coming next – this will help them to guess the meaning of the word.

or

Ask them to go back to the beginning of the sentence and start again.

If the word is still not right after two prompts then say "The word is . . ."

Notes

INTRODUCTION

1 Meek (1980).
2 Smith, B. in Styles, Bearne and Watson (1992).
3 Ibid.
4 Suggested by Frank Smith (1985) as being the most effective way of using phonics.
5 Olson (1977).
6 The research took place in an outer London comprehensive where a considerable number of children were described as having special educational needs.

   Two groups of 11-year-old poor readers (Phase 1 contained 5 children, Phase 2, 6 children) were investigated over a period of three years. These children were identified through interview and the recommendation of their primary school teacher as being children who were experiencing considerable difficulty in reading (see Figure 42).

   Each child was paired with a non-professional volunteer who helped them to compose and read a story during an 80-minute period once a week for eight weeks. Pupils were interviewed before the sessions began in order to get some idea of their views of reading and of themselves as readers.

   Interactions occurring between the non-professional scribe/listener and the composer/reader were monitored by tape recordings of each session. In order to get another viewpoint volunteers were asked to keep an informal diary noting their reactions to the sessions.

1: Sample group Phase 1					2: Sample group Phase 2				
Name	Age	R.D.	B.D.	Anx.	Name	Age	R.D.	B.D.	Anx.
Darren	11.3	*		*	Graham	11.1	*	*	*
Corinna	11.1	*	*	*	Lisa	11.4	*		*
Andrew	11.10	*	*	*	Paul	11.1	*		*
Wayne	11.3	*	*		Mandy	11.3	*	*	*
Robert	11.7	*		*	Jason	11.3	*	*	*
					Dawn	11.1	*	*	*

Key: R.D. = Reading difficulties B.D. = Some behaviour difficulties Anx. = Anxious about reading

Figure 42 Age and ability of children in two sample groups

The reading behaviour of the pupils was monitored by using a mis-cue analysis in order to see whether there were changes in the use of cueing strategies by the readers. Self-corrections were also noted as indicating an increase in independence in reading (Clay 1969, 1972b, 1991).

The simple measure of Kellog Hunt's Mean Terminal Unit (MTU) (McKenzie and Kernig 1975) was used to analyse the stories to see whether there was an increase in the complexity of the stories over the period of the eight sessions.

Analysis of data in phase 2

Pre- and post-research interviews took place with the pupils. Interviews post research with some of the volunteers allowed the triangulation of views already evident in their fuller diary entries to be expanded. Mis-cue analysis and the incidence of self-correction was again used as a measure of changes in reading behaviour.

Volunteers were encouraged to ask the composers whether they wanted to edit their stories (Sulzby 1980) and the occasions and reasons for editing were noted.

In the second phase particular concentration was given to the products of the composing sessions. A paradigm for the description of the discourse of the dictated story was found in the work of Chafe (1982, 1985), Chafe and Danielwicz (1987) and Tannen (1984, 1985). The structure of the dictated story, and its place in the continuum between oral and written stories, was described with reference to Brewer's description of universal features in the schema of oral and written stories (Brewer, 1985). This analysis has allowed some features of the discourse and structure of dictated stories to be described (Figures 43 and 44).

1 LEARNING TO READ: THE CONTEXT FOR QUESTIONS

1 HMI Reports on Reading (1991). Barry Steirer (1991) gives an excellent review of the issues relating to reading and the media and political pressures.
2 See Goswami and Bryant (1990) and Bradley and Bryant (1985).
3 Bennett (1982, 1983), Hall (1987), McKenzie (1986), Waterland (1985) and particularly Margaret Meek (1991) all describe and evaluate these movements towards an apprenticeship in reading.
4 The work of van Allen (1976), van Allen and Lee (1963), Hall (1978), Stauffer (1980) and Veatch *et al.* (1973) described the impetus that this approach had in the USA. Large-scale projects in California and Arizona in 1966, which compared the progress of children using different initial reading materials, led to the recognition of Language Experience as a major initial approach to reading. It was evaluated, along with other methods, in the First grade through to Third grade studies which compared, measured and contrasted the progress of children in order to see which methods of teaching reading were viable and effective (Dykstra 1968).
5 Hall (1985) gives a thorough historical overview of the Language Experience approach to reading.
6 Britton (1983) has an interesting reflection of his grand-daughter's use of narrative.
7 Michael (1986) has explored this idea in his small book *Purposeful Drawing*.
8 Bereiter (1979).
9 Clay (1980). Clay (1991) describes her Reading Recovery programme which

Talk	Dictated stories	Writing
Sentences		
Unfinished	Complete	Complete
'on the fly'	Time for change/reflection	Redrafting/conferencing in process model of writing
Determined by intonation or idea units	Scribes determined from composers' intonation	Extended/elaborated
Mostly conjoined with 'and'	Complete sentences mostly conjoined some subordinated	Conjoined and subordinated
Hedges and pauses Overlap between speakers	Clarification in partnership with scribe	Form and content flow together
Vocabulary		
Colloquial		Conservative
Unreferenced items Inconsistent noun/verb agreement	Dialect interference	Literary
Limited vocabulary	Some literary words and phrases	Large repertoire
Contraction	Contraction used in dialogue	
Limited choice due to time pressure	Limited choice when dictating but able to reflect/change	Time to choose
Cohesion		
Achieved paralinguistically	Intonation/thread of the story indicates cohesion	Cohesion lexicalised
Focus: ways of achieving involvement or detachment focus		
Redundancy Repeated constructions rhythm	Some elements of repeated constructions and motifs in dictated stories	'Conflating the parallel construction by eliminating the repeated parts' (Chafe 1987)
Involvement Message focused Affective/emotional	Sense of audience creating effect Intending shared emotion and feeling	Detachment and information focus in transactional writing
	Literary narrative which 'tells' a story	

Figure 43 Findings from research describing differences between talk and writing

Oral structure	Dictated stories	Written structure
Opening procedure		
Conventionalised	Usually conventional	Arbitrary
Closing procedure		
Conventionalised	Usually conventional	No convention
Sense of reprise	Sometimes reprise	Ties ends together
		Can work backwards to
		affect plot/character
Context		
Can be assumed	Rarely detailed	Must be made explicit
Can be set	Sometimes shared	Needs lexicalising
Performed in shared	Context assumed	
social context		
Narrator		
Person doing telling	Usually consistent	Any character
Can intrude on story	1st or 3rd person	Often told in 3rd person
	Occasionally mixed	past tense
Character		
Conventionalised	Little character definition	Characters fully defined
Character is 'performed'	Names appropriate	Internal processes
	Some characters defined	accessible to reader
	by dialogue	
	Few internal processes	
Action defines character	Action defines character	Action and characters
		interact
Events and episodes		
Sequential – follow order	Sequential – discourse	Can be moved in time
of underlying event	follows event structure	and sequence to create
structure	No flashforward or back	effect
Repetition occurs to aid		Flashforward and flash-
recall		back occur

Figure 44 Findings from research describing differences between oral and written story structure and the place of the dictated story

has UK government support. There are clear analogies with the Language Experience approach in the child-centred, carefully matched and monitored approach used by Clay. She also advocates a time spent at the beginning of each session reading together a well-known and loved book chosen by the child.

10 Peters and Smith (1993) cover this issue in detail in the light of both research and classroom management and resources.

11 APU report (1988).

2   THE ORGANISATION AND PRACTICALITIES OF USING THE LANGUAGE EXPERIENCE APPROACH TO LEARNING TO READ

1 Wells (1987) and Wells and Nicholls (1985).
2 Lawrence (1973). Lawrence has shown how supportive relationships with an interested adult can affect reading performance.
3 Applebee and Langer (1983). The study relates the structuring role taken by an adult in some learning situations to Halliday's five criteria for natural language learning: intentionality, appropriateness, structure, collaboration and internalisation.
4 See the work of Gillett and Gentry (1983) for an interesting description of using dictated texts for teaching forms of Standard English.
5 The taxonomy derived from the research showed the following categories:

   A *Specific composer/scribe interactions*
   1 Planning
   2 Story making
   3 Changing/discussing
   4 Reflecting
   5 Evaluating
   B *Specific reader/listener interactions*
   1 Response to correct reading
   2 Response to difficulties whilst reading
   3 Evaluating/comparing
   4 Editing/clarifying
   5 Planning
   C *Cueing*
   1 Task recall
   2 Behaviour reminder
   3 Time reminder
   D *Personal interactions where these occurred during, or as part of, the dictating/ reading part of the session*
   1 Historical (about myself)
   2 Confidential (relating to a problem)
   3 Conflict
   4 Information exchanges

6 Research into composition has shown that judicious questioning can move an apparently finished story forward. See Burtis *et al.* (1983).
7 Lawrence (1973).

3   LEARNING TO READ

1 The condition of 'learned helplessness' is acquired by internalising attitudes of negativity and dependency because of failure and difficulties in learning situations.
2 Downing (1970b) and Reid (1966). The kinds of questions asked by Downing and Reid were considered and the sample group in the research were asked what they thought reading was, what it was for. Questions were asked about why they thought they had found it difficult and how they set about dealing with a word or words they couldn't read. The same kind of cognitive confusion

identified by earlier researchers seemed to exist, with perhaps the most classic answer to the question of how you do it still being John's "I sounds it out Miss. And every time I sounds it out I get it wrong"! Older children who find reading difficult seemed to know 'sounding out' and 'pronouncing', 'spellout' and 'split up' strategies but sometimes sometimes seemed to be able to say the sounds of the letters but not synthesise them into a word, e.g. two readers could say f..l..a..g but one said it was frog and the other couldn't make it into a word at all. Overdependence in the form of 'asking' was also apparent. By 11 years of age these readers knew the relevant strategies but were not able to use them to make sense of the letters and words on the page.

3 Glynn (1980) and Glynn *et al.* (1979).

4 The use of self-correction (Clay 1969, 1972b, 1991) as an indication that a child is becoming a reflective and efficient reader has been criticised by Thompson (1984) who suggests that such self-corrections can be seen to be a result of premature response which does not allow for complete processing. His argument is persuasive and some element of impulsive and premature reading was apparent in the research samples. The powerful argument for attending to self-corrections can, however, be seen in another way as an indicator that the reader is beginning to know that predictions must make sense. When the awareness that what they are reading does not make sense causes readers to stop and self-correct then it seems obvious that they are on the way to autonomous and independent reading behaviour. The simple expedient of taking a percentage of corrected errors of the total number of errors was seen to be a sufficient indicator for the purposes of showing increased independence. In Phase 1 note was not made of differences between self-corrections which were made after the volunteer had asked a question or indicated that the response was not the expected response and self-corrections which were self-initiated.

5 The way in which volunteers tried to help pupils with phonic cueing – perhaps reflecting their own remembered strategies from school – was not always helpful and attempts to sound out sometimes resulted in a loss of meaning. On the other hand pupils spoke of their renewed confidence and the way they stuck at trying out difficult words instead of giving up. This raises the question of whether there is an interim phase in learning to use the grapho-phonic system effectively where the reader has to concentrate on the phonic construction without checking that it makes sense.

4 LEARNING THE LANGUAGE OF WRITING

1 Stauffer (1980) suggests that this is the case – making the point that what is said can be written and what is written can be read. Whilst cogent in its certainty the caution of Lawrence Holdaway (1979) that readers of these texts may be processing only limited and ultimately boring texts should perhaps also be heeded. It was a conviction raised by experience, and subsequently ratified by the research findings, that dictated stories gave insight into linguistic knowledge about written texts that extends the influence and importance of these texts beyond just 'writing down' what children say to enabling writers to compose beyond their performative writing capacity.

2 Chafe (1982, 1985), Chafe and Danielwicz (1987), Tannen (1982a, 1984, 1985).

3 Chafe and Danielwicz (1987).

4 Danielwicz (1984) found that young writers tended to go from conjoined sentences to short sentences with punctuation and little conjoining or subordinating.

Danielwicz notes that the children in her small sample group used 40 per cent more conjoining structures than the adults in their conversation. She suggests that children retain these basic structures of spoken language in their writing and that when they begin to shift from the use of conjoining as a major strategy they use relatively short, independent sentences in their writing. Studies of writing would suggest that this is an interim stage of writing in which the writer is beginning to learn to cope with the technical demands of spelling, handwriting and syntactical construction.

5 McKenzie and Kernig (1975) give a simple formula for measuring the complexity of spoken language. An attempt was made to use this version of Kellog Hunt's Mean Terminal Unit (MTU) as a measure of complexity. Central to this measure is the length of the sentence.

It has been useful as a measurement indicating ways in which composers developing some of the skills of writing through dictating stories come to use more complex constructions within sentences. Of more interest, however, was a closer examination of the kinds of subordination and embedding devices that the composers had available to use. The measurement of the complexity of a dictated story seems to bear little relationship to coherence or the handling of ideas at semantic level.

6 Perera (1986).

7 Kroll and Anson (1983) refer to such deliberate staccato sentences as a use of diction and consider it to be an aspect of literary quality in a story.

8 Chafe and Danielwicz (1987).

9 It might be expected that these would occur more frequently in the dialogue in the stories than in the body of the story; on the other hand the relative literary inexperience of these novice older composers may mean that such incoherencies and spoken qualities might occur in the text because they lack the knowledge of how written text should be. Some examples of 'bad grammar' could certainly, in these New Town children, be examples of dialect forms acceptable at a spoken level. In this category would be likely to occur such forms as 'writ' for 'wrote', 'come' or 'comed' instead of 'came', etc. Reference, and agreement in verb and antecedent, are important elements in the cohesion of the whole text.

10 Tannen (1985). It is in Tannen's discussion of the way in which some discourse is involvement focused – depending on an interpersonal response – and some is information focused, that insights have been found which help to describe the dictated story. Tannen suggests that imaginative literature has more in common with spontaneous conversation than it has with typical school writing which is minimally contextualised and which has to depend to a great degree on the writing itself in order to convey the message the writer wants to give. Imaginative literary writing, on the other hand, depends on creating a shared context with the reader and, Tannen suggests, incorporates features which are thought to be 'quintessentially literary' but that are also elements which can be seen to be basic to spontaneous conversation.

She cites:

repetition of sound (alliteration and assonance)
repetition of words
recurrent metaphors and other figures of speech
parallel syntactic constructions
compelling rhythm

as being basic ways in which speakers keep the attention of their listeners and develop their response to the message the speaker is giving. She concludes

that literary language 'builds on and perfects' these features of conversation because it is, like conversation, 'dependent for its effect on interpersonal involvement'.
11 Margaret Meek suggests in 'Play as paradox' (1985) that small children will invent words to encompass a particular excitement or pleasure in expressing what they want to say.
12 Tannen (1985).
13 Chafe and Danielwicz (1987).

5 LEARNING TO ORGANISE AND TELL A STORY

1 The analysis of children's told stories by Applebee (1978) and in particular William Brewer's (1985) comparison of oral and told stories were useful for considering the place of the dictated story. Brewer identifies a number of features of stories that allow for comparison and these were taken as the framework for looking at dictated stories.
2 Tannen (1985).
3 Chafe (1987) suggests that a high incidence of personal pronouns is an indication of the involvement of the teller and listener in conversation. In Applebee's study (1978) the youngest children told stories mainly in the first person, but by 8 or 9 years of age the request to "tell me a story" produced almost entirely third person, past tense narratives.
4 Applebee (1978) discusses the question of closeness or distance in the plots of the stories told by his, and other researchers', samples of children. Applebee also suggests that some subjects need to be distanced because of the complexity that would occur in the story, and the difficulties that would arise in dealing with this complexity, if the teller needs to deal with material which would alter a child's central constructs and expectations about life. By distancing unacceptable actions it may be easier for the story teller to explore them.
5 Britton (1983).
6 Kroll and Anson (1983) cite characterisation as one of the elements in a story, additional to the story schemata, that creates quality in the writing. Applebee (1978) suggests that in mature narratives it is often the complexity of the central character that acts as the fulcrum through which events and relationships are both conceived and structured. Chatman (1978) refers to the construct made by the reader which creates character from indications that the reader receives from the text. Rimmon-Kenan (1983) calls character a 'paradigm of traits'.
7 Bettleheim (1976) discusses the importance of vicarious engagement with emotions and fears through stories.
8 Applebee (1978).
9 Kroll and Anson (1983) found the same within their sample group. In oral stories the discourse structure usually follows the sequence of the underlying event structure. Parallel events and repetition are often used as memory markers to orientate teller and listener in the sequence. Luthi's (1984) laws of three and two to a scene also assist in the organisation and remembering of a story. Some episodes in oral stories are conventionalised, the events they describe differ from similar events in real life whilst still retaining a sequence in imagined time. Such conventionalised events in Western oral stories, Brewer (1985) suggests, could be the rescuing of the princess from a dragon and the danger inherent in wishes that come true.
10 Rosen (1988).

7 WAYS FORWARD: MAINTAINING PROGRESS AND PROGRESSING INTO OTHER ASPECTS OF LITERACY

1 Frank Smith (1984).
2 See Peters and Smith (1993).
3 Clay (1991).

Bibliography

Allen, Roach van (1976) *Language Experiences in Communication*, Boston: Houghton Mifflin.

Allen, Roach van and Lee, D. (1963) *Learning to Read through Experience*, New York: Appleton-Century-Crofts.

Applebee, A. (1977) 'A sense of story', *Theory into Practice* 16(5), pp.342–347.

Applebee, A. (1978) *The Child's Concept of Story*, Chigaco: The University of Chicago Press.

Applebee, A. and Langer, J. (1983) 'Instructional scaffolding: reading and writing as natural language activities', *Language Arts* 60(2), pp.168–175.

APU (Assessment of Performance Unit) (1988) *Language Performance in Schools: Review of APU Monitoring 1979–83*, London: HMSO.

Arnold, H. (1982) *Listening to Children Reading*, London: Hodder & Stoughton.

BBC video (1992) *Teaching Reading*.

Bennet, J. (1982) *Learning to Read with Picture Books*, Exeter: The Thimble Press.

Bennett, J. (1983) *Reaching Out: Stories for the Reader of 6-8*, Exeter: The Thimble Press.

Bereiter, C. (1979) 'Development in writing' in L. Gregg and E. Steinberg (eds) *Cognitive Processes in Writing*, Hillsdale N.J.: Lawrence Erlbaum Associates.

Bereiter, C. and Scardamalia, M. (1981) 'From conversation to composition: the role of instruction in a *developmental process*' in R. Glaser (ed.) *Advances in Instructional Psychology*, Vol. 2, Hillsdale N.J.: Lawrence Erlbaum Associates.

Bereiter, C. and Scardamalia, M. (1988) 'Children's difficulties in learning to compose' in G. Wells and J. Nicholls (eds) *Learning: An Interactional Perspective*, Lewes: Falmer Press.

Bettleheim (1976) *The Uses of Enchantment*, London: Thames & Hudson.

Britton, J. (1983) 'Writing and the story world' in B. Kroll and G. Wells (eds) *Explorations in the Development of Writing*, Chichester: John Wiley & Sons.

Brewer, W. (1985) 'The story schema: universals and cultural specific properties' in D. Olson, N. Torrance and A. Hildyard (eds) *Literacy, Language and Learning*, Cambridge: Cambridge University Press.

Bruner, J. (1990) *Acts of Meaning*, Harvard: Harvard University Press.

Bryant, P. and Bradley, L. (1985) *Children's Reading Problems*, Oxford: Basil Blackwell.

Burgess, T. (1977) 'Telling stories: what the young writer does' in M. Meek, A. Warlow and G. Barton (eds) *The Cool Web*, Chichester: John Wiley & Sons.

Burtis, P., Bereiter, C., Scardamalia, M. and Tetroe, J. (1983) 'The development of planning in writing' in B. Kroll and G. Wells (eds) *Explorations in the Development of Writing*, Chichester: John Wiley & Sons.

Chafe, W. (1980) 'The deployment of consciousness in production of a *narrative*' in W. Chafe (ed.) *The Pear Stories: Cognitive, Cultural and Linguistic Aspects of Narrative Production*, Norwood, N.J.: Ablex.

Chafe, W. (1982) 'The integration and involvement in speaking, writing and oral literature' in D. Tannen (ed.) *Spoken and Written Language*, Norwood, N.J.: Ablex.

Chafe, W. (1985) 'Linguistic differences produced by differences between speaking and writing' in D. Olson, N. Torrance and A. Hildyard (eds) *Literacy, Language and Learning*, Cambridge: Cambridge University Press.

Chafe, W. and Danielwicz, J. (1987) *The Properties of Written and Spoken Language*, Berkeley: University of California.

Chatman, S. (1978) *Story and Discourse*, New York: Cornell University Press quoted in S. Rimmon-Keenan (ed.) *Narrative Fiction*, London: Methuen.

Chomsky, C. (1978) 'If you can't read after eighth grade – what next?' in H. Samuels (ed.) *Reading and Classroom Research*, UKRA.

Clark, M. (1976) *Young Fluent Readers*, London: Heinemann Educational.

Clay, M. (1969) 'Reading errors and self-correction behaviour' in *British Journal of Educational Psychology* 39, pp.47–56.

Clay, M. (1972a) *The Early Detection of Reading Difficulties: A Diagnostic Survey*, London: Heinemann Educational.

Clay, M. (1972b) *Reading: The Patterning of Complex Behaviour*, London: Heinemann Educational.

Clay, M. (1980) 'Early writing and reading: reciprocal gains' in M. Clark and T. Glynn (eds) *Reading and Writing for the Child with Difficulties*, Educational Review Occasional Publications No. 8, Birmingham: University of Birmingham.

Clay, M. (1991) *Becoming Literate: The Construction of Inner Control*, Auckland: Heinemann.

Cox, B. and Sulzby, E. (1984) 'Children's use of reference in told, dictated and hand written stories', *Research in the Teaching of English* 18(4), Dec. 1984.

Danielwicz, J. (1984) 'The interaction between text and context: a study of how adults and children use spoken and written language in four contexts' in A. Pellengrini and T. Yawkey (eds) *The Development of Oral and Written Language in Social Contexts*, Vol. XIII in the series *Advances in Discourse Processes*, ed. R. Freedle, Norwood, N.J.: Ablex.

Dixon, C. (1977) 'Language Experience stories as diagnostic tools', *Language Arts* (54), pp.501–505.

Dobson, L. N. (1985) 'Learning to read by writing: a practical program for reluctant readers', *Teaching Exceptional Children* 18(1), pp.30–36.

Donaldson, M. (1978) *Children's Minds*, Glasgow: Hodder & Stoughton.

Downing, J. (1970a) 'Relevance versus ritual in reading' in *Reading* 4(ii), pp.4–12.

Downing, J. (1970b) 'Children's concepts of language in learning to read', *Educational Research* 12, pp.106–112.

Dykstra, R. (1968) 'Summary of the second grade phase of the co-operative research program in primary reading instruction', *Reading Research Quarterly*, Fall 1968, IV(1).

Emig, J. (1982) 'Writing composition and rhetoric' in H. Mitzel (ed.) *Encyclopaedia of Educational Research* Vol. 4, New York: The Free Press.

Gillett, J. and Gentry, S. (1983) 'Bridges between non-standard and standard English with extensions of dictated stories', *The Reading Teacher* 36(4), pp.360–364.

Glynn E. L. and McNaughton, S. S. (1975) 'Trust your own observations: criterion referenced assessment of reading progress', *Slow Learning Child* 22(2), pp.91–107.

Glynn, T. (1980) 'Parent child interaction in remedial reading at home' in M. Clark and T. Glynn (eds) *Reading and Writing for the Child with Difficulties*, Educational Review Occasional Publications No. 8, Birmingham: University of Birmingham.

Glynn, T., McNaughton, S., Robinson, V. and Quinn, M. (1979) *Remedial Reading at Home: Helping You to Help Your Child*, Wellington, New Zealand: N.Z. Council for Educational Research.

Goodman, K. (1969) 'Analysis of oral reading miscues', *Reading Research Quarterly*, Fall 1969, V(1), pp.9–30.

Goodman, K. (1976) 'Miscue analysis: theory and reality in reading' in D. Boakes and B. O'Rourke (eds) *New Directions for Reading Teaching*, Selected Proceedings of the 5th New Zealand Conference and 5th World Congress on Reading, Wellington: New Zealand Educational Institute.

Goodman, K. (1979) *Miscues: Windows on the Reading Process*, ERIC Clearinghouse on Reading and Communication Skills, Illinois: National Council of Teachers of English.

Goodman, K. and Burke, C. (1972) *Reading Miscue Inventory*, New York: Macmillan.

Goswami, U. (1990) *Phonological Skills and Learning to Read*, Hove: Lawrence Erlbaum Associates.

Goswami, U. and Bryant, P. (1990) *Phonological Skills and Learning to Read*, Hove: Lawrence Erlbaum Associates.

Grabe, M. and Grabe, C. (1985) 'The microcomputer and the Language Experience approach', *The Reading Teacher*, February 1985, pp.508–511.

Hall, M. (1972) *The Language Experience Approach for the Culturally Disadvantaged*, Newark, DE: International Reading Association.

Hall, M. (1978) *The Language Experience Approach for Teaching Reading: A Research Perspective*, Newark, DE: International Reading Association.

Hall, M. (1985) 'Focus on language experience learning and teaching', *Reading* 19(1), pp.5–12.

Hall, N. (1987) *Emergent Literacy*, London: Hodder & Stoughton in association with UKRA.

Hardy, B. (1975) *Tellers and Listeners*, University of London: Athlone Press.

Hardy, B. (1977) 'Towards a poetics of fiction: an approach through narrative' in M. Meek, A. Warlow and G. Barton (eds) *The Cool Web*, London: The Bodley Head.

Harrison, C. and Cole, M. (1992) *The Reading for Real Handbook*, London: Cassell.

Heath, S. Brice (1983) *Ways with Words: Language, Life and Work in Communities and Classrooms*, Cambridge: Cambridge University Press.

HMI (1991) *The Teaching and Learning of Reading in Primary Schools*, London: DES.

Holdaway, L. (1979) *The Foundations of Literacy*, London: Heinemann.

Johnson, T. (1977) 'Language Experience: we can't all write what we can say', *The Reading Teacher* 31(3), pp.297–300.

Kroll, B. (1983) 'Antecedents of individual differences in children's writing attainment' in B. Kroll and G. Wells (eds) *Explorations in the Development of Writing*, Chichester: John Wiley & Sons.

Kroll, B. and Anson, C. (1983) 'Analysing structure in children's fictional narrative' in H. Cowie (ed.) *The Development of Children's Imaginative Writing*, New York: St Martin's Press.

Lawrence, D. (1973) *Improved Reading Through Counselling*, London: Ward Lock.

Luthi, M. (1984) *The Fairy Tale as Art Form and Portrait of Man*, Bloomington: Indiana University Press.

MacKay, D., Thompson, B. and Schaub, P. (1978) *Breakthrough to Literacy*, London: Longman.

McDermott, R. P. (1977) 'The ethnography of speaking and reading' in R. Shuy (ed.) *Linguistic Theory: What Can it Say About Reading?*, Newark, DE: International Reading Association.

McKenzie, M. (1986) *Journeys into Literacy*, Huddersfield: Schofield & Sims.

McKenzie, M. and Kernig, W. (1975) *The Challenge of Informal Education*, London: Darton, Longman & Todd.

Mallon, B. and Berglund, R. (1984) 'The Language Experience approach to reading', *The Reading Teacher* May 1984, pp.867–871.

Meek, M. (1980) 'Prologomena for a study of children's literature' in M. Benton (ed.) *Approaches to Children's Literature*, Southampton: Southampton University, Dept of Education.

Meek, M. (1982) *Learning to Read*, London: The Bodley Head.

Meek, M. (1985) 'Play as paradox' in G. Wells and J. Nicholls (eds) *Language and Learning: An Interactional Perspective*, Lewes: Falmer Press.

Meek, M. (1988) *How Texts Teach what Readers Learn*, Exeter: The Thimble Press.

Meek, M. (1991) *On Being Literate*, London: The Bodley Head.

Michael, B. (1986) *Purposeful Drawing*, Glasgow: Jordanhill College.

Morrison, V. B. (1983) 'Language Experience reading with the microprocessor', *The Reading Teacher*, January 1983.

Olson, D. (1977) 'From utterance to text: the bias of language in speech and writing', *Harvard Educational Review* 47(3).

Perera, K. (1984) *Children's Writing and Reading: Analysing Classroom Language*, Oxford: Blackwell.

Perera, K. (1986) 'Grammatical differentiation between speech and writing in children aged 8 to 12' in A. Wilkinson (ed.) *The Writing of Writing*, Milton Keynes: Open University Press.

Perera, K. (1987) *Understanding Language*, National Association of Advisers in English.

Peters, M. L. (1985) *Spelling Caught or Taught: A New Look*, London: Routledge & Kegan Paul.

Peters, M. L. (1986) 'Purposeful writing' in B. Raban (ed.) *Practical Ways to Teach Writing*, London: Ward Lock Educational.

Peters, M. L. and Smith, B. (1986) 'The productive process: an approach to literacy for children with difficulties' in B. Root (ed.) *Resources for Reading: Does Quality Count?*, London: Macmillan Educational.

Peters, M. and Smith, B. (1993) *Spelling in Context: Strategies for Teachers and Learners*, London: NFER/Nelson.

Primary Language Record (1986) London: Centre for Primary Language in Education.

Reid, J. (1966) 'Learning to think about reading', *Educational Research* 9(1), pp.62–65.

Reimer, B. (1983) 'Recipes for Language Experience stories', *The Reading Teacher* January 1983, pp.396–401.

Rimmon-Kenan, S. (1983) *Narrative Fiction*, London: Methuen

Rosen, B. (1988) *And None of It was Nonsense*, London: Mary Glasgow Publications.

Rosen, H. (1985) *Stories and Meanings*, London: National Association for the Teaching of English.

Scardamalia, M. and Bereiter, C. (1985) 'Development of dialectical processes in composition' in D. Olson, N. Torrance and A. Hildyard (eds) *Literacy, Language and Learning*, Cambridge: Cambridge University Press.

Smith, B. M. (1981) *Silent Conversations*, Unpublished dissertation for MA in English in Education: London University Institute of Education.

Smith, B. M. (1983) 'Silent conversations: observations of secondary pupils using a Language Experience approach to reading' in B. Gillham (ed.) *Reading through the Curriculum*, London: Heinemann Educational for United Kingdom Reading Association.

Smith, B. M. (1990) *Evaluating the use of Dictated Stories as Reading Text for Poor Readers in Secondary Schools*, unpublished Ph.D. dissertation, University of Middlesex.

Smith, B. M. (1992) 'Come to my surprisement: children composing stories' in M. Styles, E. Bearne and V. Watson (eds) *After Alice: Exploring Children's Literature*, London: Cassell.

Smith, B. M. (1994) 'Finding a voice: an exploration of the stories that girls dictate' in M. Styles, E. Bearne and V. Watson (eds) *Beyond Words*, London: Cassell.

Smith, F. (1984) *Reading like a Writer*, University of Reading: Centre for Teaching of Reading in conjunction with Abel Press, Victoria B.C.

Smith, F. (1985) *Reading* (2nd edn), Cambridge: Cambridge University Press.

Smith, N. J. (1985) 'The word processing approach to Language Experience', *The Reading Teacher* February 1985, pp.556–559.

Stauffer, R. (1980) *The Language Experience Approach to the Teaching of Reading*, New York: Harper & Row.

Steirer, B. (1983) 'A researcher reading teachers reading children reading' in M. Meek (ed.) *Opening Moves*, Bedford Way Papers No. 17, London: Heinemann Educational.

Steirer, B. (1985) 'School reading volunteers', *Journal of Research in Reading* 8(1), pp.21–23.

Steirer, B. (1991) 'Assessing reading standards: a continuing debate', *Cambridge Journal of Education* 21(2).

Sulzby, E. (1980) 'Using children's dictated stories to aid comprehension', *The Reading Teacher* April 1980, pp.772–778.

Sulzby, E. (1982) 'Oral and written language mode adaptations in stories by kindergarten children', *Journal of Reading Behaviour* 14(1), pp.51–59.

Sulzby, E. (1985a) 'Kindergarteners as writers and readers' in M. Farr (ed.) *Advances in Writing Research*, Vol. 1, Norwood, N.J.: Ablex.

Tannen, D. (1982a) 'The oral/literate continuum in discourse' in D. Tannen (ed.) *Spoken and Written Language: Exploring Orality and Literacy*, Norwood, N.J.: Ablex.

Tannen, D. (1984) *Conversational Style: Analyzing Talk Among Friends*, Norwood, N.J.: Ablex.

Tannen, D. (1985) 'Relative focus on involvement in oral and written discourse' in D. Olson, N. Torrance and A. Hildyard (eds) *Literacy, Language and Learning*, Cambridge: Cambridge University Press.

Tannen, D. (1986) *That's Not What I Meant*, London: J.M. Dent.

Thompson, G. (1984) 'Self-correction and the reading process: An evaluation of evidence', *Journal of Research in Reading* 7(1), pp.53–61.

Thorogood, L. and Raban, B. (1985) 'Fostering development in the writing of 8 year olds', *Reading* 9(2), pp.100–109.

Torrance, N. and Olson, D. (1984) 'Oral and literate competencies in the early school years' in D. Olson, N. Torrance and A. Hildyard (eds) *Literacy, Language and Learning*, Cambridge: Cambridge University Press.

Veatch, J., Sawicki, F. and Elliott, G. (1973) *Keywords for Reading: the Language Experience Approach Begins*, Columbus, Ohio: Charles Merrill.

Vygotsky, L. S. (1962) *Thought and Language* (trans. G. Vakar), Cambridge, Mass.: M.I.T. Press.

Warner, S. Ashton (1963) *Teacher*, London: Penguin.

Waterland, L. (1985) *Read with Me: An Apprenticeship Approach to Reading*, Exeter: The Thimble Press.

Wells, G. (1987) *The Meaning Makers*, London: Heinemann Educational.

Wells, G. and Chang, G. (1986) 'From speech to writing: some evidences on the relationship between oracy and literacy' in A. Wilkinson (ed.) *The Writing of Writing*, Milton Keynes: Open University Press.

Wells, G. and Nicholls, J. (1985) *Language and Learning: an Interactional Perspective*, Lewes: Falmer Press.

Wray, D. (1992) 'Professional knowledge for the teaching of reading: the three S's', *Reading* 26(2), pp.2–6.

Index

achievement, gaining sense of 91
adult, and child's emotional
	problems 33, 35; role in learning to
	read 26, 38; role in reading
	maintenance 113–14 *see also*
	helpers; scribing
Allen, Roach van 140 n.4
amanuensis *see* scribing
Anson, C. 145 n.7, 146 nn.6,9
anxiety, in late readers 38
Applebee, A. 68, 143 n.3, 146 n.1, 146
	nn.3,4,6
Arnold, H. 127
Ashton-Warner, Sylvia 1
assessment, criterion-referenced 8,
	122–9; self-assessment 128–9
audience, acquiring sense of 5, 46,
	51, 54–9, 66, 118
authors, children as 8, 77, 91
autobiography, in dictated stories
	61–2, 72, 77–9

behaviour, problems 23, 38, 41, 89,
	91, 92
Bennett, J. 140 n.3
Bereiter, C. 12
Bettleheim, B. 146 n.7
books, accessibility 7–8, 36, 84; for
	beginning readers 95–6; of
	children's writing 8, 10, 37;
	production 21–2; transfer from
	dictated texts 132–3 *see also* picture
	books; texts, dictated
Bradley, L. 140 n.2
Bradley, P. 140 n.2
Breakthrough activities 116
Brewer, William 60, 139 n.6, 146
	nn.1,9

Britton, J. 65, 140 n.6
Bryant, P. 140 n.2

case studies 84, 86–94, 96–7, 98,
	99–105
Chafe, W. 48, 139 n.6, 144 nn.2,3, 146
	n.3
characters in dictated texts 67–73,
	77–9; and conventions 67;
	developing 80–1; differentiation
	69, 71–2; naming 69; number 70
Chatman, S. 146 n.6
children, attitudes to reading 37–8;
	bilingual 108, *109*, *110*, 114; with
	severe difficulties 44
Chomsky, Carol 99
clarification, need for 51, 54, 70, 75,
	104
Clarke, M. 98
classroom projects 84–100;
	collaboration 99–105; with Down's
	Syndrome child 91–2; with
	dyslexic children 94–5; infants,
	individual texts 88–90, small
	groups 85–8, 99–101; junior school
	101; necessary components 84, *85*;
	secondary school 92–4, 95–6;
	short-term 91; strategies for
	problems 96–9
Clay, M. 12, 119–21
cohesion, in talk 54; in writing 55
collaboration, *see* group work
colloquialisms, in written texts 52–4,
	58, 62
comics, in reading maintenance 113
communication, as purpose of
	writing 95
composing *see* writing